When Christmas Comes . . .

When Christmas Comes . . .

An Anthology of
Childhood Christmases

compiled by
ANNE HARVEY

SUTTON PUBLISHING

First published in the United Kingdom in 2002 by
Sutton Publishing Limited · Phoenix Mill
Thrupp · Stroud · Gloucestershire · GL5 2BU

British Library Cataloguing in Publication Data
A catalogue record for this book is available from the British
Library.

ISBN 0-7509-2805-0

Typeset in 11/16.5pt Sabon.
Typesetting and origination by
Sutton Publishing Limited.
Printed and bound in England by
J.H. Haynes & Co. Ltd, Sparkford.

Contents

SANTA CLAUS AND STOCKINGS

In the Week when Christmas Comes

Eleanor Farjeon

This is the week when Christmas comes,
Let every pudding burst with plums,
And every tree bear dolls and drums,
In the week when Christmas comes.

Let every hall have boughs of green,
With berries glowing in between,
In the week when Christmas comes.

Let every doorstep have a song
Sounding the dark street along,
In the week when Christmas comes.

Let every steeple ring a bell
With a joyful tale to tell,
In the week when Christmas comes.

Let every night put forth a star
To show us where the heavens are,
In the week when Christmas comes.

Let every pen enfold a lamb
Sleeping warm beside its dam,
In the week when Christmas comes.

This is the week when Christmas comes.

Preface

Chill December brings the sleet,
Blazing fire and Christmas treat.

This is the final couplet in 'The Months', the poem written by
Sara Coleridge for her 3-year-old son in 1841.

The word 'Christmas' immediately evokes childhood. I don't
believe, as I've heard said, that 'Christmas is just for the
children', but I do believe that at Christmas time we can
recapture the spirit of childhood. In this widely celebrated
festival, and at the centre of Christian belief, at the close of the
year, is a child, the Christ Child.

For me, Christmas 2001 went on until Easter 2002, because
when everyone else had dismantled the tree, sent the cards for
recycling, taken down the decorations, disposed of unwanted
presents and left overs and finished the thank-you letters, I was
still compiling this anthology. While children were back in
uniform for the new school term and Valentine cards and
daffodils were appearing, I was deep in nostalgic memories of
Christmas, choosing seasonal poems and excerpts, poring over
pictures of angels and robins, snowmen, stars and Santa Claus.
This was a new experience, and through January, February and
March I felt comfortably cut-off from reality. It was a warm,
privileged time, although shadowed, I must admit, by knowing
that a wealth of material would have to be left out.

Decisions had to be made. I wanted the anthology to draw
on the many facets of a child's expectation and experience: the

food and the presents, the preparation, the enigma of Father Christmas, the knobbly stocking, the magical tree, the sense of wonder as well as those moments of fear and disappointment.

An anthology is a kind of cake or pudding or stocking, filled with assorted ingredients. Or perhaps it resembles a pie: I hope, like Jack Horner, you will find some plums in mine.

Anne Harvey
2002

Puddings and Pies

Little Jack Horner
Sat in a corner,
Eating a Christmas pie;
He put in his thumb
And pulled out a plum,
And said, What a good
boy am I!

The real Jack Horner was possibly the steward of the Abbot of Glastonbury
who, wanting to appease Henry VIII, sent a pie containing, not an edible
plum, but the deeds of twelve manors. The plum pudding itself has a long
history and dates back to the seventeenth century. Traditionally, 'Stir-up
Sunday' is the last Sunday before Advent, when the Church of England collect
begins, 'Stir up, we beseech thee, O Lord, the wills of thy faithful people . . .'.
This was interpreted as a reminder to 'stir-up' the mixture for Christmas
puddings and pies, giving them time to mature. Children were taught to use
only a wooden spoon and to stir the pudding clockwise . . . Everyone present
must have a stir, in order of seniority.

Stir up, we beseech thee,
The pudding in the pot,
And when it is ready
We'll eat it piping hot.

There are not so many round, cannon-like puddings nowadays, boiled in a cloth with steam filling the kitchen, and today's mincemeat is meat-less, but we can still believe that any man, woman or child who eats twelve mince pies in twelve different houses during the twelve days of Christmas, will be happy from January to December the following year.

Illustration by Quentin Blake, from *Hogmanay and Tiffany*.

Pudding Charms

Charlotte Druitt Cole

Our Christmas pudding was made in November,
All they put in it, I quite well remember:
Currants and raisins, and sugar and spice,
Orange peel, lemon peel – everything nice
Mixed up together, and put in a pan.
'When you've stirred it,' said Mother, 'as much as you can,
We'll cover it over, that nothing may spoil it,
And then, in the copper, to-morrow we'll boil it.'
That night, when we children were all fast asleep,
A real fairy godmother came crip-a-creep!

She wore a red cloak, and a tall steeple hat
(Though nobody saw her but Tinker, the cat!)
And out of her pocket a thimble she drew,
A button of silver, a silver horse-shoe,
And, whisp'ring a charm, in the pudding pan popped them,
Then flew up the chimney directly she dropped them;
And even old Tinker pretended he slept
(With Tinker a secret is sure to be kept!)
So nobody knew, until Christmas came round,
And there, in the pudding, these treasures we found.

from Days at Wickham

Anne Viccars Barber

Anne Viccars Barber followed her famous Buxton ancestors, who included
Elizabeth Fry, in recording and illustrating childhood experiences.
Her book Days at Wickham *reveals some delightful*
Christmas memories.

Quite a long time before Christmas Nanny makes the Christmas puddings. We take it in turns to stir and make a wish. I always have a battle with myself as I long to wish for a lovely doll but instead I wish that my mother's indigestion would get better. I do the same when I am lucky enough to have the wishbone of the chicken. I do wish her indigestion would hurry up and get better so that I could have the wish for myself.

From Mince Pies for Christmas, 1805.

Christmas Plum Pudding

Clifton Bingham

When they sat down that day to dine
The beef was good, the turkey fine
But oh, the pudding!

The goose was tender and so nice,
That everybody had some twice –
But oh, that pudding!

It's coming, that they knew quite well,
They didn't see, they couldn't smell,
That fine plum pudding!

It came, an object of delight!
Their mouths watered at the sight
Of that plum pudding!

When they had finished, it was true,
They'd also put a finish to
That poor plum pudding!

from Father and Son

Edmund Gosse

Edmund Gosse recalls the Christmas following his mother's death in 1857,
when he was eight years old.

My Father's austerity of behaviour was, I think, perpetually
accentuated by his fear of doing anything to offend the
consciences of these persons, who he supposed, no doubt, to be
more sensitive than they really were. He
was fond of saying that 'a very little
stain upon the conscience makes a
wide breach in our communion
with God,' and he counted
possible errors of conduct by
hundreds and by thousands. It
was in this winter that his
attention was particularly
drawn to the festival of Christmas, which, apparently, he had
scarcely noticed in London.

On the subject of all feasts of
the Church he held views of an
almost grotesque peculiarity. He
looked upon each of them as nugatory and
worthless, but the keeping of Christmas appeared to him by far
the most hateful, and nothing less than an act of idolatry. 'The
very word is Popish,' he used to exclaim, 'Christ's Mass!'
pursing up his lips with the gesture of one who tastes
assafoetida by accident. Then he would adduce the antiquity of
the so-called feast, adapted from horrible heathen rites, and

itself a soiled relic of the abominable Yule-Tide. He would denounce the horrors of Christmas until it almost made me blush to look at a holly-berry.

On Christmas Day of this year 1857 our villa saw a very unusual sight. My Father had given strictest charge that no difference whatever was to be made in our meals on that day; the dinner was to be neither more copious than usual nor less so. He was obeyed, but the servants, secretly rebellious, made a small plum-pudding for themselves. (I discovered afterwards, with pain, that Miss Marks received a slice of it in her boudoir.) Early in the afternoon, the maids, – of whom we were now advanced to keeping two, – kindly remarked that 'the poor dear child ought to have a bit, anyhow,' and wheedled me into the kitchen, where I ate a slice of plum-pudding. Shortly I began to feel that pain inside which in my frail state was inevitable, and my conscience smote me violently. At length, I could bear my spiritual anguish no longer, and bursting into the study I called out: 'Oh! Papa, Papa, I have eaten of flesh offered to idols!' It took some time, between my sobs, to explain what had happened. Then my Father sternly said: 'Where is the accursed thing?' I explained that as much as was left of it was still on the kitchen table. He took me by the hand, and ran with me into the midst of the startled servants, seized what remained of the pudding, and with the plate in one hand and me still tight in the other, ran till we reached the dust-heap, when he flung the idolatrous confectionery on to the middle of the ashes, and then raked it deep down into the mass. The suddenness, the violence, the velocity of this extraordinary act made an impression on my memory which nothing will ever efface.

Mincemeat

Elizabeth Gould

Sing a song of mincemeat,
Currants, raisins, spice,
Apples, sugar, nutmeg,
Everything that's nice,
Stir it with a ladle,
Wish a lovely wish,
Drop it in the middle
Of your well-filled dish,
Stir again for good luck,
Pack it all away
Tied in little jars and pots,
Until Christmas Day.

Banana Mincemeat

*A recipe for children's parties from a 1930s
women's magazine*

This is light and delicate, and makes a change from the ordinary kind. Skin 6 large bananas and mash them. Grate the rind of 2 lemons and squeeze their juice, chop 6 oz. of suet; mix all these together with 6oz. of currants, and a tablespoonful of orange-flower water; sugar may be added to taste, but ¼ lb will be about the right quantity. This mincemeat is best used quickly, and should be tied down with bladder or vegetable parchment.

Menu for a King

Eleanor Farjeon

In The New Book of Days, *published in 1941, Eleanor Farjeon provided a scrap of fun or fancy, fact or fable for every day of the year. The book proved invaluable to school teachers . . . and to anthology editors.*

The Country was France. The Year, 1611. The King was ten years old. And this was what he had for dinner.

Corinth raisins in rose water.

Egg soupe with lemon juice, 20 spoonsful.

Broth, 4 spoonsful.

Cocks combs, 8.

A little boiled chicken.

4 mouthfuls of boiled veal.

The marrow of a bone.

A wing and a half of chicken, roasted and then fried in bread crumb.

13 spoonsful of jelly.

A sugar horn filled with apricots.

Half a sugared chestnut in rose water.

Preserved cherries.

A little bread and some fennel comfits.

The fennel comfits were for the little King's digestion.

Mrs Beeton called the turkey 'a noble dish, roast or boiled', and added 'A Christmas dinner with the middle classes of this empire would scarcely be a Christmas dinner without its turkey and we can hardly imagine an object of greater envy than is presented by respected portly paterfamilias carving, at the season devoted to good cheer and genial charity, his own fat turkey, and carving it well.'
One wonders if that portly father's children ever gave a tender thought for the turkey's plight, as today's children might . . . and as American poet, Shel Silverstein certainly does.

Point of View

Shel Silverstein

Thanksgiving dinner's sad and thankless
Christmas dinner's dark and blue
When you stop and try to see it
From the turkey's point of view.

Sunday dinner isn't sunny
Easter feasts are just bad luck
When you see it from the viewpoint
Of a chicken or a duck.

Oh how I once loved tuna salad
Pork and lobsters, lamb chops too
Till I stopped and looked at dinner
From the dinner's point of view.

The poet and artist, Colin West, imagines that even the Christmas Cake has feelings.

The Father Christmas on the Cake

Colin West

For fifty weeks I've languished
Upon the cupboard shelf,
Forgotten and uncared for,
I've muttered to myself.
But now the year is closing,
And Christmastime is here,
They dust me down and tell me
To show a little cheer.
Between the plaster snowman
And little glassy lake
They stand me in the middle
Of some ice-covered cake,
And for a while there's laughter,
But as the week wears on,

They cut up all the landscape
Till every scrap is gone.
Then with the plaster snowman
And little lake of glass
I'm banished to the cupboard
For one more year to pass.

Illustration by Quentin Blake, from *Hogmanay and Tiffany*.

Traditional Rhyme

Without the door let sorrow lie,
And if for cold it hap to die
We'll bury it in a Christmas Pie
And evermore be merry.

Giving and Getting

A little gift by friendship's hand conferred
Is often to the costliest gem preferred . . .

from The Girls' Friend

Children should make it a rule to prepare Christmas presents for their families. Even the youngest can offer something. For weeks before the important day you should be as busy as little bees, contriving and making such things as you suppose to be most agreeable. . . . There will be a great deal of hiding and whispering, of course. Little girls who exercise their ingenuity in making boxes, baskets and needlecases etc. for Christmas will find their hearts warmed with good feeling, and discover, as the Bible tells, that 'IT IS MORE BLESSED TO GIVE THAN TO RECEIVE.'

For Them

Eleanor Farjeon

Before you bid, for Christmas' sake,
Your guests to sit at meat,
Oh please to save a little cake
For them that have no treat.

Before you go down party-dressed
In silver gown or gold,
Oh please to send a little vest
To them that still go cold.

Before you give your girl and boy
Gay gifts to be undone,
Oh please to spare a little toy
To them that will have none.

Before you gather round the tree
To dance the day about,
Oh please to give a little glee
To them that go without.

'Toys for Poor Children', from *My Pet's Album* by Robert Barnes.

from Little Women

Louisa M. Alcott

This story, published in 1868, was based on the author's own family life. When I was about thirteen we acted the play version at my drama classes. I had to be Meg, but, like most girls, longed to be the tomboy, Jo. . . . who, of course, was Louisa herself. Here is an extract from Chapter One, Playing Pilgrims.

'Christmas won't be Christmas without any presents,' grumbled Jo, lying on the rug.

'It's so dreadful to be poor!' sighed Meg, looking down at her old dress.

'I don't think it's fair for some girls to have plenty of pretty things, and other girls nothing at all,' added little Amy, with an injured sniff.

'We've got father and mother and each other,' said Beth, contentedly from her corner.

The four young faces on which the firelight shone brightened at the cheerful words, but darkened again as Jo said sadly:

'We haven't got father, and shall not have him for a long time.' She didn't say 'perhaps never', but each silently added it, thinking of father far away, where the fighting was.

Nobody spoke for a minute; then Meg said in an altered tone:

'You know the reason mother proposed not having any presents this Christmas was because it is going to be a hard winter for everyone; and she thinks we ought not to spend money for pleasure when our men are suffering so in the army. We can't do much, but we can make our little sacrifices, and ought to do it gladly. But I am afraid I don't'; and Meg shook her head, and she thought regretfully of all the pretty things she wanted.

Shirley Hughes' illustration of Jo, Meg, Beth and Amy, with
Marmee, for the 1953 Puffin edition of *Little Women*.

'But I don't think the little we should spend would do any
good. We've each got a dollar, and the army wouldn't be much
helped by our giving that. I agree not to expect anything from
mother or you, but I do want to buy *Undine and Sintram* for
myself; I've wanted it *so* long,' said Jo, who was a bookworm.

'I planned to spend mine on new music,' said Beth, with a
little sigh, which no one heard but the hearth-brush and kettle-
holder.

'I shall get a nice box of Faber's drawing pencils; I really need
them,' said Amy, decidedly. . . .

'Merry Christmas, Marmee! Many of them! Thank you for our books; we read some, and mean to, every day,' they cried, in chorus.

'Merry Christmas, little daughters! I'm glad you began at once, and hope you will keep on. But I want to say one word before we sit down. Not far away from here lies a poor woman with a little new-born baby. Six children are huddled into one bed to keep from freezing, for they have no fire. There is nothing to eat over there; and the oldest boy came to tell me they were suffering hunger and cold. My girls, will you give them your breakfast as a Christmas present?'

They were all unusually hungry, having waited nearly an hour, and for a minute no one spoke; only a minute, for Jo exclaimed impetuously:

'I'm so glad you came before we began!'

'May I go and help carrying the things to the poor little children?' said Beth, eagerly.

'*I* shall take the cream and the muffins,' added Amy, heroically, giving up the articles she most liked.

Meg was already covering the buckwheats, and piling the bread into one big plate.

'I thought you'd do it,' said Mrs March, smiling as if satisfied. 'You shall all go and help me, and when we come back we will have bread and milk for breakfast, and make it up at dinner-time.'

They were soon ready, and the procession set out. Fortunately it was early, and they went through back streets, so few people saw them, and no one laughed at the queer party.

A poor, bare, miserable room it was, with broken windows, no fire, ragged bed-clothes, a sick mother, wailing baby, and a group of pale, hungry children cuddled under one old quilt, trying to keep warm.

How the big eyes stared and blue lips smiled as the girls went in!

Operation Christmas Child

Samaritan's Purse International is an organisation that sends shoe boxes, decorated with Christmas paper and filled with gifts to children in war-torn, Third World countries. The project 'Operation Christmas Child' grows yearly, with heart-warming responses. Each November finds me begging my local shops for shoe boxes, so that my grandchildren and I can decorate and fill them with gifts. These stories are from their Operation Shoe Box Report.

Vukovar shoe boxes

I have loads of stories but I cry too much when I tell them. The children were delighted. I have never seen such delight on children's faces. Everyone said how lucky they were that God had sent us.

As we were leaving an orphanage at Osijek after delivering the boxes, a teenage boy stood at the door to say goodbye. He had broken up the large bar of Dairy Crunch chocolate that he had received in his box into small pieces and wanted to give us each a piece as we left. He was so proud to be able to give us something; it was very humbling.

In another orphanage I spent some time with 1–5-year-olds. A little boy had received a recorder in his box and I sat with him on the floor to show him how to blow and make a noise. The look on his face was incredible. He thought it was wonderful.

I feel quite emotionally drained but wouldn't have missed that for the world.

Love, Sandra Reynolds

Stories from Georgia

Anna is an orphan just 8 years old from South Georgia. When she received her OCC box she began to cry. We asked why and she explained that God had told her in a dream that she would soon receive a present from her mum. So when we gave her the shoe box she thought her dream had come true. She was overcome with emotion.

Number of shoe boxes from UK and Ireland up to 18th Feb 2002	
Afghanistan	19,267
Albania	18,798
Armenia	61,855
Azerbaijan	61,875
Belarus	77,519
Bosnia	41,666
Bulgaria	17,263
Croatia	47,050
Czech Republic	17,481
Georgia	61,622
Hungary	70,858
Kosovo	20,460
Macedonia	32,745
Poland	18,946
Romania	243,246
Russia	85,730
Serbia	180,829
Ukraine	65,557
Total 1,142,767	

George's Story

George is an orphan, but he has three brothers and sisters. When George found gloves, a hat and a scarf in his box he asked, 'How did God know that he and his brothers desperately needed gloves?' He told us that the one pair of gloves would be worn in shifts so that all four children would get a turn!

Barnardo boys in waiting: three six-year-olds and one bear at the Hove Home, 1954.

Stories from Croatia

A young boy received a shoe box meant for a 10–14-years-old girl because the shoe boxes for 9-year-old boys had run out. In the box was a pair of pearl drop earrings which Stuart offered to exchange for something else. The little boy declined saying, 'for mama, for mama'. Later, when he re-opened his box, he repeated, 'for mama' and seemed delighted.

A teenage girl received a hat that was much too small, but she too refused the offer to exchange the gift. 'No, for baby brother' was her response.

Two 14-year-old girls when given their boxes took them to their bedrooms and put the contents together so that they could share each other's gifts.

In 1969 Kaye Webb edited a special anthology for Puffin Books in aid of the Save the Children Fund. The book included the following extracts:

from *The Friday Miracle*

From a small Korean boy to his sponsor in Edinburgh

My thanks that you have sent the money. I am now become a pair of trousers, two under-trousers and two warm shirts. . . . I am very happy.

From a schoolboy in Lesotho (Africa)

Kind Friends, It was to my greatest surprise when I received some parcel present from you. My gratitude is beyond the utmost reach of human thought and there is no words to express. Could I tabulate the things I bought with it, you would be shocked with pleasure.

I have bought by it these are the things: a bag for carrying my school books; books, a blazer and a full school uniform. As I fail to hit on the right verb to express my great thanks I think all my gratitude should be expressed in four words which I think they are not little as far as I am concerned. The great words are – 'thank you very much'.

Tonio's Gift

Five-year-old Tonio was chosen to be the youngest shepherd in the Nativity play. The children were asked to bring a present for the babe in the manger. Tonio, whose family was very poor, brought his most precious possession, a piece of wood, worn smooth with handling. It was his only toy, which he had kept hidden and played with in secret, otherwise it would have been taken from him and used for firewood. He wept a little as he parted with it.

A visitor, hearing the story of his gift, sent a beautiful red engine to Tonio in place of his piece of wood. Beaming with delight, Tonio tip-toed to the crib and retrieved his piece of wood, leaving the beautiful red engine in its place.

Fond mother (shaking her Johnnie by the collar) to welfare worker after Christmas festivities: 'I 'opes he said 'thank you' for 'is present, Miss; I'm that pertickeler about 'is manners. 'Gawd luv 'us, I ses when he come 'ome, 'not *annuver* bleedin' present' I ses!' (*Eve Garnett*)

from Three Houses

Angela Thirkell

Every adult can sympathise with the child who, soon after Christmas, is made to sit down and write thank-you letters. Angela Thirkell, granddaughter of the artist Edward Burne-Jones, recalled in her autobiography:

After a decent interval the Curse of Christmas descended upon us in the shape of thank-you letters. My brother and I had written a quantity of blank forms in trusting anticipation of a good haul of presents, more or less in this form:

Dear . . .,

Thank you very much for the . . . It is a lovely . . . and thank you so much for it. I hope you had a very happy Christmas. Your loving . . .

But unluckily a rather hurried caligraphy made 'much' look like 'muck' and most of the thank-you forms were confiscated and destroyed. What a brooding nightmare thank-you letters are to children. One can't tell them not to write, but when I get letters from my nieces more or less as follows:

Dear Aunt Anglia (or Angelia),

Thank you so much for the lovely necklace. It was a lovely necklace and I do like it so much. We had a lot of presents. Now I must stop with love from Mary,

my heart aches for the tedious time they have spent on this and other thank-you letters.

23

Christmas Thank-You's

Mick Gowar

Dear Auntie
Oh, what a nice jumper
I've always adored powder blue
and fancy you thinking of
orange and pink
for the stripes
how clever of you!

Dear Uncle
The soap is terrific
So
useful and such a kind thought and
how did you guess that
I'd just used the last of
the soap that last Christmas brought

Dear Gran
Many thanks for the hankies
Now I really can't wait for the flu
and the daisies embroidered
in red round the 'M'
for Michael
how
thoughtful of you!

Dear Grandad
Don't fret
I'm delighted
So don't think your gift will
offend
I'm not at all hurt
that you gave up this year
and just sent me
a fiver
to spend

Dear Cousin
What socks!
and the same sort you wear
so you must be
the last word in style
and I'm certain you're right that the
luminous green
will make me stand out a mile

Dear Sister
I quite understand your concern
it's a risk sending jam in the post
But I think I've pulled out
all the big bits
of glass
so it won't taste too sharp
spread on toast

Afterthought

Elizabeth Jennings

For weeks before it comes I feel excited, yet when it
At last arrives, things all go wrong:
My thoughts don't seem to fit.

I've planned what I'll give everyone and what they'll give to me,
And then on Christmas morning all
The presents seem to be

Useless and tarnished. I have dreamt that everything would come
To life – presents and people too.
Instead of that, I'm dumb,

And people say, 'How horrid! What a sulky little boy!'
And they are right. I *can't* seem pleased.
The lovely shining toy

I wanted so much when I saw it in a magazine
Seems pointless now. And Christmas too
No longer seems to mean

The hush, the star, the baby, people being kind again.
The bells are rung, sledges are drawn,
And peace on earth for men.

A Christmas Conundrum

Herbert Farjeon

In the 1930s, Herbert Farjeon, writing for the Humorist, *quizzed readers with conundrums. Here is one of them:*

Two days after Christmas a small boy with a very keen sense of honour receives an exciting looking parcel on the outside of which is written:

'IMPORTANT! NOT TO BE OPENED BEFORE CHRISTMAS!'

If the small boy insists on keeping the parcel intact for 363 days, should his parents pat him on the head for his upright conduct? Or should they slap him and tell him not to be such a frightful little idiot?

Santa Claus and Stockings

Christmas Stocking

Eleanor Farjeon

What will go into the Christmas Stocking
While the clock on the mantelpiece goes tick-tocking?
    An orange, a penny,
    Some sweets, not too many,
    A trumpet, a dolly,
    A sprig of red holly,
    A book and a top
    And a grocery shop,
    Some beads in a box,
    An ass and an ox
    And a lamb, plain and good,
    All whittled in wood,
    A white sugar dove,
    A handful of love,
    Another of fun,
    And it's very near done –
    A big silver star
    On top – there you are!
Come morning you'll wake to the clock's tick-tocking,
And that's what you'll find in the Christmas Stocking.

A Christmas Annual, 1919.

On 21 September 1897, the editor of the New York Sun received this letter from Virginia O'Hanlon and gave what has now become the classic reply to all children who ask, 'Is there really a Santa Claus?'

Dear Editor – I am eight years old. Some of my little friends say there is no Santa Claus. Papa says 'If you see it in "The Sun" it's so.' Please tell me the truth, is there a Santa Claus?

The editor replied:

Virginia, your little friends are wrong. They have been affected by the skepticism of a skeptical age. They do not believe except they see. Yes, Virginia, there is a Santa Claus. Alas! how dreary would be the world if there were no Santa Claus! It would be as dreary as if there were no Virginias. There would be no childlike faith then, no poetry, no romance to make tolerable this existence. We should have no enjoyment except in sense and sight. The external light with which childhood fills the world would be extinguished.

Not believe in Santa Claus! You might as well not believe in fairies!

Nobody sees Santa Claus, but that is no sign that there is no Santa Claus. The most real things in the world are those that neither children nor men can see. Did you ever see fairies dancing on the lawn? Of course not, but that's no proof that they are not there. Nobody can conceive or imagine all the wonders there are unseen and unseeable in the world.

No Santa Claus! Thank God he lives forever! A thousand years from now, Virginia, nay, ten times ten thousand years from now, he will continue to make glad the heart of childhood.

The Night Before Christmas

Clement C. Moore

One of the most famous Christmas poems of all is Clement Clarke Moore's 'A visit from St Nicholas', often called by its sub-title, 'The Night Before Christmas'. The story behind its long life merits a book of its own.

It is claimed, certainly in America, that Santa Claus, his sleigh, reindeer, habits of pipe-smoking and descending the chimneys of all 'good' boys and girls, originated with this poem, although one must not forget the real St Nicholas, who was born in Patara in Turkey, around 270 AD. It was said that he stood up and joined his hands in prayerful thanksgiving on the day of his birth, and even refused his mother's breast on feast days. Many tales are told about him, and his feast day, celebrated in some countries, is 6 December. He was adopted as patron saint of Russia, and in Holland, the patron saint of children. Try saying 'St Nicholas' over and over again and you will see how Santa Claus emerged.

Clement Clarke Moore, born in rural old New York in 1779, was a clever hard-working student who spoke numerous languages. His hobbies included writing verse and playing the violin. He was appointed Professor of Oriental and Greek literature in the General Theological Seminary, and he and his wife, Catherine, had nine children. The first few will have enjoyed their father's jolly verses, as he read them aloud in 1822. His Santa Claus was supposedly based on the family's plump and jovial Dutch handyman, and it was while being driven home one night that the jingling bells on the horse inspired the poem.

The following year it was sent, anonymously, to a local newspaper, published without the author's consent, and eagerly copied by many fascinated readers. It was as late as 1838 that Moore received recognition for his work.

Wood engraving by T.C. Boyd from the first
illustrated edition of the poem, 1848.

'Twas the night before Christmas, when all through the house
Not a creature was stirring, not even a mouse;
The stockings were hung by the chimney with care,
In hopes that St Nicholas soon would be there;
The children were nestled all snug in their beds,
While visions of sugarplums danced in their heads;

And Mamma in her 'kerchief', and I in my cap,
Had just settled our brains for a long winter's nap;
When out on the lawn there arose such a clatter,
I sprang from the bed to see what was the matter.
Away to the window I flew like a flash,
Tore open the shutters and threw up the sash.

The moon, on the breast of the new-fallen snow,
Gave the lustre of midday to objects below,
When what to my wondering eyes should appear,
But a miniature sleigh, and eight tiny reindeer,
With a little old driver, so lively and quick,
I knew in a moment it must be St Nick.

More rapid than eagles his courses they came,
And he whistled and shouted, and called them by name;
'Now, Dasher! Now, Dancer! Now, Prancer and Vixen!
On, Comet! On, Cupid! On, Donner and Blitzen!
To the top of the porch! To the top of the wall!
Now, dash away! Dash away! Dash away all!'

As dry leaves that before the wild hurricane fly,
When they meet with an obstacle, mount to the sky;
So up to the housetop the coursers they flew,
With the sleigh full of toys, and St Nicholas, too.
And then, in a twinkling, I heard on the roof
The prancing and pawing of each little hoof –
As I drew in my head, and was turning around,
Down the chimney St Nicholas came with a bound.

He was dressed all in fur, from his head to his foot,
And his clothes were all tarnished with ashes and soot;
A bundle of toys he had flung on his back,
And he looked like a pedlar just opening his pack.
His eyes – how they twinkled! His dimples, how merry!
His cheeks were like roses, his nose like a cherry!

His droll little mouth was drawn up like a bow,
And the beard of his chin was as white as the snow;
The stump of a pipe he held tight in his teeth,
And the smoke it encircled his head like a wreath;
He had a broad face and a little round belly
That shook, when he laughed, like a bowl full of jelly.

He was chubby and plump, a right jolly old elf,
And I laughed, when I saw him, in spite of myself;
A wink of his eye and a twist of his head,
Soon gave me to know I had nothing to dread;
He spoke not a word, but went straight to his work,
And filled all the stockings; then turned with a jerk,

And laying his finger aside of his nose,
And giving a nod, up the chimney he rose;
He sprang to his sleigh, to his team gave a whistle,
And away they all flew like the down of a thistle.
But I heard him exclaim, ere he drove out of sight,
'Happy Christmas to all, and to all a good night!'

The Night After Christmas

Anne P.L. Field

This sequel, published in an American anthology early in the twentieth century, might well inspire a further parody, and introduce today's worldly infant, complete with computer, e-mail and mobile phone.

'Twas the night after Christmas in Santa-Claus land
And to rest from his labours St. Nicholas planned.
The reindeer were turned out to pasture and all
The ten thousand assistants discharged till the fall.
The furry great-coat was laid safely away
With the boots and the cap with its tassel so gay,
And toasting his toes by a merry wood fire,
What more could a weary old Santa desire?
So he puffed at his pipe and remarked to his wife,
'This amply makes up for my strenuous life!
From climbing down chimneys my legs fairly ache,
But it's well worth the while for the dear children's sake.
I'd bruise every bone in my body to see
The darlings' delight in a gift-laden tree!'

Just then came a sound like a telephone bell –
Though why they should have such a thing I can't tell –
St. Nick gave a snort and exclaimed in a rage,
'Bad luck to inventions of this modern age!'
He grabbed the receiver – his face wore a frown
As he roared in the mouth-piece, 'I will not come down
To exchange any toys like an up-to-date store,
Ring off, I'll not listen to anything more!'
Then he settled himself by the comforting blaze
And waxed reminiscent of halcyon days

When children were happy with simplest of toys:
A doll for the girls and a drum for the boys –
But again came that noisy disturber of peace
The telephone bell – would the sound never cease?

'Run and answer it, wife, all my patience has fled,
If they keep this thing up I shall wish I were dead!
I have worked night and day the best part of a year
To supply all the children, and what do I hear –
A boy who declares he received roller-skates
When he wanted a gun – and a cross girl who states
That she asked for a new Victor talking machine
And I brought her a sled, so she thinks I am 'mean!'
Poor St Nicholas looked just the picture of woe,
He needed some auto-suggestion, you know,
To make him thinks things were all coming out right,
For he didn't get one wink of slumber that night!
The telephone wire was kept sizzling hot
By children disgusted with presents they'd got,
And when the bright sun showed its face in the sky
The Santa-Claus family were ready to cry!
Just then something happened – a way of escape,
Though it came in the funniest possible shape –
An aeronaut, sorely in need of a meal,
Descended for breakfast – it seemed quite ideal!
For the end of it was, he invited his host
Out to try the balloon, of whose speed he could boast.
St. Nick, who was nothing if not a good sport,
Was delighted to go, and as quick as a thought
Climbed into the car for a flight in the air –
'No telephone bells can disturb me up there!
And, wife, if it suits me I'll count it no crime
To stay up till ready for next Christmas time!'
Thus saying – he sailed in the giant balloon,
And I fear that he will not return very soon.
Now, when you ask 'Central' for Santa-Claus land
She'll say, 'discontinued' – and you'll understand.

from Knickerbocker's History of New York

Washington Irving

Although Clement Moore is credited with creating the image of Father Christmas, it is another American, Washington Irving, who wrote, in Knickerbocker's History of New York *in 1809, fourteen years before the famous poem:*

The good St Nicholas would often make his appearance in his beloved city of a holiday afternoon, riding jollily above the tree tops or over the roofs of the houses, now and then drawing forth magnificent presents from his breeches pockets and dropping them down the chimneys of his favourites. Whereas in these degenerate days of iron and brass he never visits us save one night in the year when he rattles down the chimneys of the descendants of patriarchs, confining his presents merely to the children in token of the degeneracy of the parents.

Christmas Day

Alison Uttley

'I was a snow-baby, a lucky baby, they said, born just before Christmas, in the great storm' wrote Alison Uttley. Born on a farm in the Derbyshire Peak District, she grew up to enchant adults and children alike with her stories. In The Country Child *the main character, Susan Garland, re-lives her own childhood.*

Susan awoke in the dark of Christmas morning. A weight lay on her feet, and she moved her toes up and down. She sat up and rubbed her eyes. It was Christmas Day. She stretched out her hands and found the knobby little stocking, which she brought into bed with her and clasped tightly in her arms as she fell asleep again.

She awoke later and lay holding her happiness, enjoying the moment. The light was dim, but the heavy mass of the chest of drawers stood out against the pale walls, all blue like the snow shadows outside. She drew her curtains and looked out at the starry sky. She listened for the bells of the sleigh, but no sound came through the stillness except the screech owl's call.

She pinched the stocking from the toe to the top, where her white suspender tapes were stitched. It was full of nice knobs and lumps, and a flat thing like a book stuck out of the top. She drew it out – it *was* a book, just what she wanted most. She sniffed at it, and liked the smell of the cardboard back with deep letters cut in it. She ran her fingers along like a blind man and could not read the title, but there were three words in it.

Next came an apple, with its sweet, sharp odour. She recognized it, a yellow one, from the apple chamber, and from her favourite tree. She took a bite with her strong, white little teeth and scrunched it in the dark.

Next came a curious thing, pointed and spiked, with battlements like a tower. Whatever could it be? It was smooth like ivory and shone even in the dark. She ran her fingers round the little rim and found a knob. She gave it a tug, and a ribbon flew out – it was a tape-measure to measure a thousand things, the trees' girths, the calf's nose, the pony's tail. She put it on her knee and continued her search.

There was a tin ball that unscrewed and was filled with comfits, and an orange, and a sugar mouse, all these were easy to feel, a sugar watch with a paper face and a chain of coloured ribbon, a doll's chair, and a penny china doll with a round smooth head. She at once named it Diana, after Diana of the Ephesians, for this one could never be an idol, being made of pot. She put her next to her skin down the neck of her nightdress, and pulled the last little bumps out of the stocking toe. They were walnuts, smelling of the orchards at Bird-in-Bush Farm, where they grew on great trees overhanging the wall, and a silver shilling, the only one she ever got, and very great wealth, but it was intended for the money-box in the hall. It was the nicest Christmas stocking she had ever had, and she hugged her knees up to her chin and rocked with joy.

What Billy Wanted

Anon

Dear Santa Claus,
You brought a sledge
To me a year ago,
And when you come again, I hope,
You'll bring along some snow,

The Perfect Stocking

Rose Henniker Heaton

Here is a suggestion from The Perfect Christmas, *published in 1932:*

A large-size golf stocking. A tangerine (wrapped in gold paper) in the toe and a tinsel ball in the heel help to preserve the shape.

A packet of Alphabet biscuits that spell 'A Happy Christmas.'

Chocolate letters that spell the owner's name.

A purse with a new sixpence in it.

A box of Dominoes.

Happy Families.

A walnut with either a thimble or toy soldier inside.

Chocolates covered in gold and silver that look like money.

A magnet.

Some wire puzzles.

A pencil sharpener like a globe of the world.

A box of chalks.

A little box of 'transfers'.

Gay crackers sticking out of the top.

The Waiting Game

John Mole

Nuts and marbles in the toe,
An orange in the heel,
A Christmas stocking in the dark
Is wonderful to feel.

Shadowy, bulging length of leg
That crackles when you clutch,
A Christmas stocking in the dark
Is marvellous to touch.

You lie back on your pillow
But that shape's still hanging there.
A Christmas stocking in the dark
Is very hard to bear,

So try to get to sleep again
And chase the hours away.
A Christmas stocking in the dark
Must wait for Christmas Day.

LET · VS · SHARE · Yᵉ · FRUIT · OF · Yᵉ · XMAS · TREE.

Santa Claus

Florence Harrison

Oh, Santa Claus, no music beats
When you are passing down the streets!
And who has heard from far away
The bells that tinkle on your sleigh,
Dear Santa Claus?

Your hand has never knocked the door,
Your foot upon the nursery floor
has never left a trace of snow;
How do you come? how do you go,
Old Santa Claus?

On Christmas Eve for girls and boys
You fill long stockings full of toys,
With many a sweet and sugar plum,
But none have ever seen you come,
Dear Santa Claus.

Oh – through the wind and snow and sleet,
Up at the pane above the street
I'd watch for you, but old folks say
When children wake, you stay away,
Dear Santa Claus.

So you must bow above my bed
This Christmas Eve, and touch my head
With kisses, soft – as shadows creep –
And I may see you in my sleep,
Dear Santa Claus.

from How to be a Little Sod

Simon Brett

*Crime writer and dramatist Simon Brett invented the beguilingly wicked
character of a baby, nicknamed affectionately (or not!) Little Sod. Having made
it clear, at birth, that he is in control, he approaches his first Christmas.*

Day 17

A new excitement today – paper chains.

Apparently we're getting near Christmas and She's clearly
going to make a very big deal of it. Don't know if She always
does, or whether it's in my honour.

As She put the paper chains up, She kept saying, 'Doesn't oo
love the uvvy paper chains then? Isn't they pretty then? Doesn't
oo like them then?'

The answer is, yes I do like them. But, needless to say, not to
look at.

As usual, my opportunity came when the phone rang. Minute
She was out the door, I crawled across to grab the end of the
paper chain She was putting up and systematically began to
shred it.

I found an unexpected ally in my efforts. The cat came and
joined in, ripping the chain into confetti. It's
the first time we've done anything together,
me and the cat. Maybe a friendly
relationship can develop between
us after all.

Maybe not, though. I,
cannier than the cat,
heard Her put the phone
down and made sure that,

by the time She was back in the room, I had crawled away to the other side and was looking disapprovingly at the poor creature. Caught red-pawed.

It got smacked fiercely and did its customary bolting-through-the-cat-flap.

It'll be quite a while before that friendly relationship develops.

Day 18

They do keep going on about this first word business. 'I'm really looking forward to hearing the baby speak,' I overheard Her murmuring rather gooily to Him this evening.

'I'm not so sure,' was His jocular reply. 'Maybe we won't like what we hear.'

There's many a true word spoken in jest. But I wouldn't be that cruel. Would I?

Mind you, it is tempting.

'And wouldn't it be lovely,' She went on, 'if the first word came out on Christmas Day . . .'

Sometimes Her naive optimism is so touching. On the other hand, why not? I'm not basically vindictive, and if my pronouncing my first word on Christmas Day is going to give harmless pleasure, why should I deny it to them?

Suppose I could say, 'Happy Christmas!' That would certainly be seasonal and appropriate.

Or I could do the full Tiny Tim routine and say, 'God bless us, every one!' Though I think that might be a bit corny.

My thoughts were interrupted by Him saying, 'Yes, that would be great. On Christmas Day. When both our parents are here . . .'

I see. It's not just for them. They want to show me off.

Day 24

Don't know what they think they were doing this evening.

There I was, happily drifting off to sleep, when in they blundered, reeling and giggling slightly (obviously been getting into the Christmas spirit early) and tied an empty stocking on to the end of my cot. Then, a bit later, in they came again and replaced it with a full one. What is this?

Now I'm quite willing to go along with the whole Father Christmas charade in a few years' time, if it makes them happy. I'll write letters to stuff up the chimney, I'll hang an empty stocking at the end of my bed, leave out a mince pie and a glass of whisky, and some crisps for the reindeer, and show amazement at the fact that my stocking has been filled by Christmas morning. But I'm not even one yet! Why on earth do they imagine that I will be able to appreciate the complex idea of a legendary benefactor who reputedly descends chimneys and philanthropically fills the stockings of well-behaved children?

Some things about my parents I will never understand.

Day 25

Christmas Day – as if I'd be allowed to forget it!

I woke up before they did and looked down to the end of my cot. Surprise, surprise – there was the stocking.

For a moment I considered falling on it and ripping out its contents. And then I thought – why make it easy for them? They can jolly well show me what to do with it.

My parents duly took me into their bed, and helped me to open my stocking. I dutifully ripped the paper off all the presents, while they cooed with delight as each one was revealed. There was something rather charming in the innocent glee on their faces.

'Oh, isn't that uvvy then?' they kept saying. 'Doesn't oo like Christmas then?'

I was tempted to use this moment for my first word. But I'm not sure that 'Humbug' would have gone down that well.

from It's Too Late Now

A.A. Milne

On Thursday 24 December 1925 a short paragraph in the Evening News *announced: 'Christopher Robin Page 7 To-Night . . . To-Morrow Night's Broadcast. A new story for children, 'Winnie-the-Pooh', about Christopher Robin and his Teddy Bear, written by Mr A.A. Milne specially for the 'Evening News', appears to-night on Page Seven. It will be broadcast from all stations by Mr Donald Calthrop, as part of the Christmas Day wireless programmes at 7.45. p.m. to-morrow.'*

Winnie-the-Pooh must appear, in book or cuddly toy form, in many a Christmas stocking. He and Christopher Robin are world famous. Less well known is A.A. Milne's 1925 autobiography which includes this memory of Christmas:

Normally we spent the Christmas holidays in London. We didn't hang up stockings on Christmas Eve. Somebody – at first supposed to be Father Christmas, but at a very early age identified with Papa – came into our room at night, and put our presents at the foot of the bed. It was exciting waking up in the morning and seeing what treasures we had got; it was maddening to know that we should not be able to enjoy them properly until we had come back from church. Was it really supposed that a child, with all his Christmas presents waiting for him, could give his mind to the herald angels?

Hark the herald angels sing
(I've never had a paint-box with tubes in before)
Glory to the new born King
(I'll paint a little cottage with a green front door)
Peace on earth and mercy mild
(My knife's a jolly good one, they've marked it Sheffield steel)
God and sinners reconciled
(I've got it in my pocket, I can feel it when I feel)
Hark the herald angels sing
(I wish it were tomorrow, I must sail my boat)
Glory to the new-born King
(I'll take it to the bathroom and just watch it float)

Letters from Fanny Longfellow

Mrs Longfellow, from a crayon
drawing by Samuel Worcester
Rowse.

Fanny, the beautiful wife of American poet, Henry Wadsworth Longfellow,
used to write to her children pretending to be Santa Claus. These letters seem
even more poignant when one learns that Fanny died when set alight by
candle flames while she was sealing her daughters' curls into small packets for
keepsakes. The little girls appear in their father's poem 'The Children's Hour':
. . . Grave Alice, and laughing Allegra,
And Edith with golden hair. . . .
A number of the Christmas letters, some of them undated, are given here.

Christmas Eve, 1851

My dear Charley,

A merry Christmas again to you, my little friend! As I peep slyly at your face upon the pillow I am very glad to see it so rosy and round, and to find you well and strong this year as last. I hope to find you as good too – much *better*, for you should keep growing good as well as strong, but I am sorry I sometimes hear you are not so kind to your little brother as I wish you were. Try to be kinder this year and more obedient to papa and mamma who love you very much and whom

Edith (left), Annie allegra (below), and Alice Longfellow, daughters of Henry Wadsworth Longfellow and Fanny Appleton Longfellow, from the painting by Thomas Buchanan Read.

you love, too, I know. I hope you won't be disappointed that I do not bring what you ask for in your letter, but the truth is I do not like to have little boys play soldiers though I don't mind their playing with them, so I fill your stocking with a watch, which will make the time pass very sweetly, and I find in my bag some beautiful books your kind friend Mr Rölker popped in as I came along which I think you will like as well.

Good night! away I go!

Your constant friend
Santi Claus

P.S. I like to see toothbrushes well used.

My darling little baby [Alice],

How are *you*? Fat, and rosy, and good as ever? Last Christmas you could only *crow* and now you can say I don't know how many words, and run about like a little mouse. You are not too little to be very affectionate and obedient either, and I think you are still one of my best little girls.

I have a beautiful bird in my bag for you who will sing to you all day long but not so well as dear little Dickey and Willy. And I give you Tom Thumb for a husband and many kisses besides before I fly away.

Good bye.
Your old loving
Santi Claus

Charles Appleton (left) and Ernest Wadsworth Longfellow, sons of Henry Wadsworth Longfellow and Fanny Appleton Longfellow, from a pastel by Eastman Johnson.

Xmas Eve 1851.

Dear Charley,

A merry Christmas to you! Is it possible I see a jacket hanging on that chair, and bless me! a waistcoat! why how you little folks do grow. But I hope you will not yet outgrow old Santa Claus, who dearly loves you though he wishes sometimes you were a little more gentle and obedient to papa and mamma.

I believe you have taken pretty good care of your teeth as I told you but I want you to keep your heart clean of bad thoughts and secret thoughts and to tell your dear mamma and papa everything you do and think. I am glad to see you have studied so well this year, but am in too great hurry to say all I would.

Your loving

Santa Claus

I forgot to give you my love and to say that I think you have been a very good boy this year.

Dear Erny,

I am very happy to see you so fat and rosy this year and to know that you no longer suck your thumb, but instead use it much better by holding a pencil by it and drawing such beautiful pictures. Why don't you try your hand upon *me* as you have taken to portraits I hear?

Good bye, darling boy. Think how many chimneys I have got to pop down.

Your loving old

Santa Claus

A Merry Christmas!

Christmas Eve 1853

Chimney Corner

Dear Charley and Erny,

I have not time tonight to write you each a letter, having so many little folks' stockings to fill and I am afraid to stay here too long for fear you should see me, for I hear you begin to find me out and that

50

will never do until you are too big to be pleased with toys and bonbons.

I love to come and wish you a merry Christmas but I wish I could say you had been as good boys this year as the last. You have not been so obedient and gentle and kind and loving to your parents and little sister as I like to have you, and you have picked up some naughty words which I hope you will throw away as you would sour or bitter fruit. Try to stop to think before you use any, and remember if no one else hears you God is always near and you would not wish to speak them before Him.

A new Year is just beginning and I hope to find you at the end of it among my best boys.

Ever your loving
Santa Claus

Struwwelpeter

Heinrich Hoffmann

Dr Heinrich Hoffmann, a Frankfurt physician, was in the habit of writing amusing verses for his small son, Carl, and drawing funny pictures for a child patient. These came together in a Christmas present for 3-year-old Carl in 1844. Struwwelpeter or 'Shock-headed Peter' is a series of poems about eight naughty boys and only one little girl! It later became one of the most popular children's books of all time, and though some were frightened by it, the good doctor's intention had been to mock the over pious, moralistic writing of the Victorian era.

THE
ENGLISH STRUWWELPETER
OR
PRETTY STORIES
AND
FUNNY PICTURES.

When the children have been good,
That is, be it understood,
Good at meal-times, good at play,
Good all night and good all day, —
They shall have the pretty things
Merry Christmas always brings.
Naughty, romping girls and boys
Tear their clothes and make a noise,
Spoil their pinafores and frocks,
And deserve no Christmas-box.
Such as these shall never look
At this pretty Picture-Book.

A Quick Note from Father Christmas

John Mole

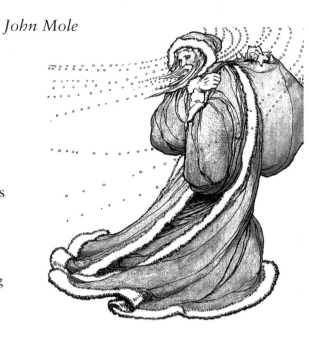

Great pie,
Thanks mate,
Got to go,
Can't wait,
So many houses
Still to visit,
Not much fun this
Really, is it?
Wife's tired too,
Wants me home,
No joke Santa-ing
On your own.

Christmas Conundrums

Herbert Farjeon

Here are two more 'Christmas Problems' for the reader to solve.

Three little brothers, two good and one bad, have been brought up by their fanciful parents to believe that their stockings really are filled by Santa Claus.

On Christmas Eve, when the three brothers are all asleep, their parents go through the annual performance of filling the stockings, two-thirds junk and one third quite desirable little presents.

A couple of hours later the bad brother, although it is not yet morning, wakes up, sees that Santa Claus has filled the stockings, hops out of bed, empties the contents of all the stockings on to the floor, collects all the nice things and stuffs them in his own stocking, puts all the junk into the stockings of his brothers, and then hops back into his bed again.

In the morning the parents find that the bad brother has all the nice things and guess at once what must have happened.

By what means, if any, is it possible for the parents to restore the balance and bring the bad brother to book without giving the Santa Claus game away?

* * * * * * *

A gentleman dressed up as Father Christmas is seen by the mistress of the household at three o'clock in the morning coming out of the parlour-maid's bedroom.

Should she call her husband?
And if so, what should she call Him?

Herbert Farjeon did not supply answers to his conundrums. The last one made me think of the once popular song

I saw Mummy kissing Santa Claus
Underneath the mistletoe last night. . . .

And that, in turn, made me recall some of the other songs that vye with Carols at Christmas-time: I'm Dreaming of a White Christmas . . . All I Want for Christmas is my two front teeth . . . Rudolf the Red-Nosed Reindeer . . . Have Yourself a Merry Little Christmas . . . Jingle Bells . . . *and many more.*
Jingle Bells and Merry Little Christmases suggest PARTIES.

Party Pieces

Children's parties alternate between being hugely successful and deeply disastrous. One can sympathise with Ogden Nash's plea:

May I join you in the doghouse, Rover?
I wish to retire till the party's over.

Despite his jaundiced viewpoint, children are filled with excitement at the thought of a party.

Home for the Holidays

Anon

We shall have sport when Christmas comes,
When 'snap-dragon' burns our fingers and thumbs:
We'll hang mistletoe over our dear little cousins,
And pull them beneath it and kiss them by dozens:
We shall have games at 'Blind Man's Buff',
And noise and laughter and romping enough.

We'll crown the plum-pudding with bunches of bay,
And roast all the chestnuts that come in our way;
And when Twelfth Night falls, we'll have such a cake
That as we stand around it the table shall quake.
We'll draw 'King and Queen', and be happy together,
And dance old 'Sir Roger' with hearts like a feather.
Home for the Holidays, here we go!
But this Fast train is really exceedingly slow!

A well-conducted party game from *Home for the Holidays*.

The One I Knew the Best of All

Frances Hodgson Burnett

The Christmas holidays, a time of great festivity, began with the 'Breaking-up Party' wrote Frances Hodgson Burnett. 'The Breaking Up', she tells us, 'was a glittering . . . a brilliant thing', and was only the beginning. 'Every little boy or girl, whose Mamma could indulge in such a luxury, gave a Christmas Party.' Hodgson Burnett writes in the third person, calling herself the Small Person, and describes the dressing up, the food, the dancing and the music, but through it all makes clear that in the end the Party failed to live up to the heightened sense of expectation and delicious anticipation.

'Is this *really* the Party?' she would say mentally. And then, to convince herself, to make it real, 'Yes, this is the *Party*. I am at the *Party*. I have my Party frock on – they are all dancing. This is the Party.'

And yet as she stood and stared, and the gay sashes floated by, she was restlessly conscious of not being quite convinced and satisfied, and of something which was saying,

'Yes – we are all here. It looks real, but somehow it doesn't seem exactly as if it was the *Party*.'

And one does it all one's life. Everybody dances, everybody hears the music, everybody some time wears a sash and a necklace and watches other White Frocks whirling by – but was there ever any one who really went to the Party?

'Will you dance this waltz with me?'

57

Mistletoe, A Charade in Three Acts

The Brothers Mayhew

Charades, played in America and England, may have derived from the French 'petits jeux'. The Brothers Mayhew insisted that 'young and old both delight in the game and no party is allowed to pass without playing them'.

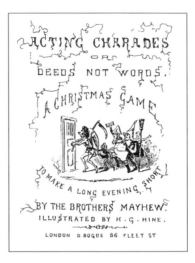

ACT I
MISTLE– (Mizzle)
DRAMATIS PERSONAE

POOR TENANT   HIS WIFE   HIS FAMILY

ANGRY LANDLORD

SCENE– *House of Poor Tenant comfortably furnished*

Enter POOR TENANT in a state of extreme dejection. HIS WIFE, who follows him, endeavours to console him, but in vain, for he only stamps and presses his forehead the more. She clings to him and demands the cause of his sorrow. He pulls from his pocket a placard written, 'RENT DAY TO-MORROW. She falls back in horror, and weeps.

58

Enter HIS FAMILY, who, seeing their Father and Mother's affliction, are overcome by their feelings. They turn aside their heads and sob audibly.

Poor Tenant addresses His Family. He a second time exhibits his placard, and the sorrow of the group becomes extreme. He tells them, by pulling his pockets out, that he has not a penny. He points to his comfortable furniture, and informs them that the Angry Landlord will seize it all for rent. Sinking into a

chair, he is overwhelmed in his grief. His Wife and Family gather round him, and ask in what way they can assist him. They offer to bear away their goods that night, and carry them beyond the reach of the Angry Landlord. A gleam of joy passes over the countenance of Poor Tenant. He embraces his children, and His Wife blesses them.

His Family then seize the chairs, and carry them on tiptoe into the passage. They return stealthily, until the whole room is stripped. Then casting a long farewell look at the ceiling of their forefathers' home – they strike a touching tableau, and *exeunt* Poor Tenant, His Wife, and Family, mournfully.

 Enter ANGRY LANDLORD, with a pen in his mouth and a ledger under his arm. He stamps loudly on the floor of Poor Tenant's house, but nobody comes. He stamps again and again, his face wearing an expression of surprise and disgust. In a great passion he raves about the room, expressing in action his indignation at all the furniture having been removed. He swears to be revenged, and draws a writ from his pocket.

Exit Angry Landlord, still wearing vengeance.

ACT II

–TOE

DRAMATIS PERSONAE

THE POPE OF ROME   CARDINALS   PRIESTS

IRISH GENTLEMAN   ENGLISH GENTLEMAN   PAPAL

SOLDIERS

SCENE – *Interior of a Chapel at Rome. Around it are hung pictures, and at the end is the arm-chair for the Pope's throne.*

Enter IRISH GENTLEMAN and ENGLISH GENTLEMAN arm-in-arm, to view the beauties of the chapel. They are both delighted with the pictures, and while the Irish Gentleman kneels down, the English one carves his name on the door, to tell all further visitors that he has been there.

The solemn music of a piano is heard, and

Enter THE POPE OF ROME, dressed in full canonicals of red table-cover and lace cuffs. He walks grandly, and is followed by CARDINALS in sacerdotal robes of bed-curtains, and devout PRIESTS in ladies' cloaks with the hoods over their heads. They tell their beads of coral necklaces.

The Pope seats himself in the arm-chair throne, and the Priests commence kissing his toe. He blesses each one as he rises. The Irish Gentleman advancing, beseeches by gestures Cardinals to allow him to take one fond embrace. They are pleased with his earnestness, and consent. He casts himself on his knees and kisses it madly.

They then invite the English Gentleman also to advance and be blessed. He folds his arms and refuses disdainfully. The Pope is enraged, and rises from his throne. The Cardinals gather menacingly round English Gentleman, and the Priests threaten him with wild gesticulations. The Irish Gentleman in vain endeavours to restore peace. His friend is once more besought to yield, but still refuses. The Pope beckons to his priests, when

Enter PAPAL SOLDIERS, and surround English Gentleman, who still remains with his arms crossed. He refuses to stir, and addresses the Pope and his Court in language of contempt. The Guards are ordered to do their duty and force English Gentleman away with the point of their brooms. (*Soft Music.*) *Exeunt* Pope, Cardinals, and Priests solemnly, the Irish Gentleman cheering.

ACT III
MISTLETOE
DRAMATIS PERSONAE
GRANDFATHER   HIS SON

GRANDMOTHER   HER DAUGHTER (*Wife to His Son*)

THEIR CHILDREN   VISITORS   SERVANTS   MUSICIANS

SCENE– *Old Hall in the Mansion of His Son. Long table down the centre, with chairs.*

Enter SERVANTS bearing grand feast, which they arrange on the table. They then stand behind the chairs.

Enter GRANDFATHER, GRANDMOTHER, HIS SON, HER DAUGHTER, THEIR CHILDREN, and VISITORS in holiday costume. Grandfather is so old he can scarcely walk, and is supported by His Son, whom he blesses. Grandmother is placed next to Her Daughter, and Their Children dance about with delight. When they are seated at table, they eat.

Enter Servants bearing large dish with brown silk bundle in it for plum-pudding. Their Children rise from the table and dance round it.

As soon as the dinner is removed, His Son gives a signal, when Enter MUSICIANS with imitation instruments in their hands. Their Children serve them with wine and plum-pudding. (*Affecting picture.*) Grandfather goes out and fetches a bunch of Mistletoe, which he hangs to the lamp. They all laugh, and are delighted with the wickedness of Grandfather. He laughs and coughs a great deal, and all Their Children thump him on the back to make him better.

The Visitors then take the Young Ladies, who appear dreadfully bashful, and drag them screaming and tittering under the Mistletoe, where they embrace them theatrically, by crossing their heads over their shoulders. Grandmother is delighted, and presses her sides with mirth, when one of Their Children takes her hand, and pulls her under the Mistletoe and kisses her. Grandfather pretends to be jealous, and the fun increases.

Several of the Gentlemen are smitten with the charms of the Ladies, and after they have kissed them, proceed to the corners, where they fall on one knee and propose. The Ladies weep, hesitate, and point to Grandfather. The Gentlemen beseech the Grandfather to consent. He weeps, and blesses them.

Muscians begin playing a court dance, all the party standing up. The old Grandfather taking Grandmother's hand, leads off the dance.

Drawing lots for charades at a children's party on Twelfth Night.

William's Christmas Eve

Richmal Crompton

Richmal Crompton's schoolboy character, William Brown, had firm views on most subjects, including parties:

It was Christmas. The air was full of excitement and secrecy. William, whose old-time faith in notes to Father Christmas sent up the chimney had died a natural death as the result of bitter experience, had thoughtfully presented each of his friends and relations with a list of his immediate requirements.

He had a vague and not unfounded misgiving that his family would begin at the bottom of the list instead of the top. He was not surprised, therefore, when he saw his father come home rather later than usual carrying a parcel of books under his arm. A few days afterwards he announced casually at breakfast:

'Well, I only hope no one gives me 'The Great Chief,' or 'The Pirate Ship,' or 'The Land of Danger' for Christmas.'

His father started.

'Why?' he said sharply.

'Jus' 'cause I've read them, that's all,' explained William with a bland look of innocence.

The glance that Mr Brown threw at his offspring was not altogether devoid of suspicion, but he said nothing. He set off after breakfast with the same parcel of books under his arm and returned with another. This time, however, he did not put them in the library cupboard, and William searched in vain.

The question of Christmas festivities loomed large upon the social horizon.

'Robert and Ethel can have their party on the day before Christmas Eve,' decided Mrs Brown, 'and then William can have his on Christmas Eve.'

William surveyed his elder brother and sister gloomily.

'Yes, an' us eat up jus' what they've left,' he said with bitterness. 'I know!'

Mrs Brown changed the subject hastily.

'Now let's see whom we'll have for your party, William,' she said, taking out pencil and paper. 'You say whom you'd like and I'll make a list.'

'Ginger an' Douglas an' Henry and Joan,' said William promptly.

Things I want for Crismus

1. A Bicycle.
2. A grammarfone.
3. A pony.
4. A snake.
5. A monkey.
6. A Bugal.
7. A trumpit
8. A red Injun uniform
9. A lot of sweets.
10. A lot of books.

'Yes? Who else?'

'I'd like the milkman.'

'You can't have the milkman, William. Don't be so foolish.'

'Well, I'd like to have Fisty Green. He can whistle with his fingers in his mouth.'

'He's a butcher's boy, William! You *can't* have him?'

'Well, who *can* I have?'

'Johnnie Brent?'

'I don't like him.'

'But you must invite him. He asked you to his.'

'Well, I didn't want to go,' he said irritably, 'you made me.'

'But if he asks you to his you must ask him back.'

'You don't want me to invite folks I don't *want*?' William said in the voice of one goaded against his will into exasperation.

'You must invite people who invite you,' said Mrs Brown firmly, 'that's what we always do in parties.'

'Then they've got to invite you again and it goes on and on and *on*,' argued William. 'Where's the *sense* of it? I don't like Johnnie Brent an' he don't like me an' if we go on inviting each other an' our mothers go on making us go, it'll go on and on and *on*. Where's the *sense* of it? I only jus' want to know where's the *sense* of it?'

His logic was unanswerable.

'Well, anyway, William, I'll draw up the list. You can go and play.'

William walked away, frowning, with his hands in his pockets. 'Where's the *sense* of it?' he muttered as he went.

from A Nursery in the Nineties

Eleanor Farjeon

In this extract Eleanor Farjeon tells the story of her London childhood. Born in 1881, she was not quite nine when the following event took place.

I was always shy at a party, and I always had a stomach ache on party-days. I wasn't pretty and I knew I wasn't; also I wore spectacles at a time when spectacles on a child made the grown-ups say 'What a pity!'

Whenever I was asked to a party I hoped I would enjoy it more than last time, I hoped I would be as gay and popular and petted as little Olive Routledge who wore lovely frocks, went to heaps of parties and danced like a fairy. Oh for Olive's confidence! I never longed for it more than in the January of 1890 when I was invited to a large party given by Mrs Charles Wyndham in her big house in St John's Wood Park. Her parties were always crowded with strange and brilliant children before whom I would be terrified to make a fool of myself by falling down on the polished slippery floor . . . Olive was, as usual, the prettiest child there . . . After tea there were some games and then the usual requests for some child to 'do' something began. There were

songs and recitations and Olive danced, picking up her lace skirts and floating like a snowflake . . . Then I heard Mrs Wyndham's voice saying in my ear, 'Nellie, I'm sure you know a little piece to recite to us.' The moment had come which I always dreaded. Could I get out of it or would I have to? I was learning a rather silly little poem with my governess which began:

> A pound of tea at one and three
> A pot of strawberry jam, Some new laid
>   eggs, some wooden pegs
> And a dozen rashers of ham.

The poem was about a little girl going shopping for her mother . . . she goes over the list, gets in a muddle and asks the grocer for the wrong things . . . I heard Mama say: 'Can you say, A Pound of Tea dear?' . . . It was no good, I would have to . . . the floor seemed very big and full of people. I wetted my lips and began: in a monotonous little voice . . .

> A pound of three at one and tea
> a pot of strawberry ham, Some new laid
>   pegs, some wooden eggs, and a dozen
>   rashers of jam . . .

Oh horror! I had said it all wrong, the jumble shouldn't begin till the third verse . . . I was not pretending to be a muddle-headed little girl, I WAS a muddle-headed little girl . . . I began again, hastily . . . A pound of tea at one and three a pot of strawberry jam . . . Then hesitated. Every line, every word of the poem went out of my head . . .

'A Pound of Tea . . . ' I began again, then faltered. Somebody said 'She's forgotten it, poor little thing'. I burst into tears, slithered along the floor polish and sobbed in Mama's lap. She tried to comfort me; some of the elders patted me and said

'Never mind dear' and another child got up and recited something competently. Oh how awful it was Oh if only I could go straight home . . . But the party went on, there were more games to play, and Sir Roger de Coverley to dance . . . I felt I would suffer every night of my life! Wherever I went I thought all the grown-ups, and all the brilliant and pretty children were pointing and whispering . . . 'That is the little girl who forgot her piece and cried! That is the little girl who forgot her piece and cried!'

The Ill-Considered Trifle

Alan Melville

Alan Melville was about the same age as the young Eleanor Farjeon, but, as you will discover in this incident from his revealing memoir, Myself When Younger, *he was far more confident and worldly.*

Monica Gibson was an inoffensive little girl of about seven with a lot of freckles who attended this particular Christmas party wearing a pale pink taffeta dress with a lot of smocking all over the front. Either it wasn't very good smocking, or Monica must have been remarkably flat-chested, because half way through tea I remember noticing that between the front of the dress and Monica there was a large gap. I was sitting next to her at the tea-table, and there was the gap and there on my plate was a fair-sized helping of rather soggy trifle, and it seemed the most natural thing in the world to do. I just scooped the lot up with my spoon and slowly and very deliberately dropped it down the gap. I had nothing against the girl; as a matter of fact, we were rather chummy because she had relatives in Malaya and used to give me the foreign stamps off their letters.

Monica watched me, fascinated, as I manoeuvred the trifle towards her with a remarkably steady hand, and it wasn't until the trifle reached wherever it did reach that she realised what was happening. She then let forth a fiendish bawl, and the grown-ups (who had been having a quiet cigarette in the next room in the mistaken conviction that I couldn't do anything really awful while there was food around)

came running from all directions to see what had happened now, for goodness' sake. Monica being incoherent because of her bawling, and the state of her party frock being in any case open to misinterpretation, it was left to a poisonous little sneak called Henry Purves who was sitting opposite to blow the gaff.

'He dropped his trifle down her frock,' he announced – which was, of course, perfectly true. 'He's *always* dropping trifle down little girls' frocks,' he added. Which was a filthy lie. It was the first time I had ever done such a thing and, as it so happens, I've never done it since.

The Magic Show

Vernon Scannell

After a feast of sausage-rolls,
Sandwiches of various meats,
Jewelled jellies, brimming bowls
Of chocolate ice and other treats,

We children played at Blind Man's Buff,
Hide-and-Seek, Pin-the-Tail-on-Ned,
And then – when we'd had just enough
Of party games – we were all led
Into another room to see
The Magic Show. The wizard held
A wand of polished ebony;
His white-gloved, flickering hands compelled
The rapt attention of us all.
He conjured from astonished air
A living pigeon and a fall
Of paper snowflakes; made us stare
Bewildered, as a playing card –
Unlike a leopard – changed its spots
And disappeared. He placed some starred
And satin scarves in silver pots,
Withdrew them as plain bits of rag,
Then swallowed them before our eyes.
But soon we felt attention flag
And found delighted, first surprise
Had withered like a wintry leaf;
And, when the tricks were over, we
Applauded, yet felt some relief,
And left the party willingly.
'Good night,' we said, 'and thank you for
The lovely time we've had.' Outside
The freezing night was still. We saw
Above our heads the slow clouds stride
Across the vast, unswallowable skies;
White, graceful gestures of the moon,
The stars' intent and glittering eyes,
And, gleaming like a silver spoon,

The Conjuror at a Victorian Christmas Party.

The frosty path to lead us home.
Our breath hung blossoms on unseen
Boughs of air as we passed there,
And we forgot that we had been
Pleased briefly by that conjuror,
Could not recall his tricks, or face,
Bewitched and awed, as now we were,
By magic of the commonplace.

*Every child knows the dread of not being picked in a team game, of coming
bottom in a quiz, voted 'last down' in Musical Bumps or the one who moved
in Statues. Such memories led Herbert Farjeon to ask:*

Is Musical Chairs Immoral?

Herbert Farjeon

Having in my time attended a number of post-Christmas
Children's Parties, I have come to the considered conclusion
that if there is one game which no nice child should be allowed
to play, that game is Musical Chairs.

If there has ever been a clean game of Musical Chairs in the whole history of the drawing-room, I have not witnessed it. For chicanery, for brutality, for backstairs methods of every kind, there is nothing to approach it.

One dodge is to take Lilliputian steps, practically marking time at a great rate, by which means the player achieves an appearance of hurrying when he is really delaying. Another – and the tiniest mites are not above this – is to pretend that your shoe-lace has come undone, and to go on tying it up, directly in front of a chair, until the pianist stays his hand.

Another trick, quickly learned by innocents not turned three, is to pretend you think that the music has stopped when it is still in progress, and to take a seat (and hold it against all comers), as it were by accident. Such a position is, I have observed, especially convenient for the sticking out of the leg and tripping up of the player behind.

Angling for position before the march begins is another revolting business. Why do you so rarely find two big boys next to one another? Because they are foxy enough to 'wangle the draw,' and to contrive sandwiching themselves between the smallest and weakest girls. With my own eyes I have seen a great hulking lout of seven push a tot of four to the ground at the crucial moment. And the darkest feature of it all is that the last thing expected by the grown-ups themselves is a display of chivalry.

When I was a small boy – to furnish an illustration – I once found myself 'last in' with a small girl who happened to be my hostess. Now it occurred to me that it would, in the circumstances, be decent to let her win; so I let her win. With my last breath I would swear that I could have won had I chosen. But I did not choose. I stood aside. And what did the grown-ups say?

They said: 'Fancy being beaten by a girl!' They said: 'You must look sharper than that if you want to get on in the world.' And I couldn't explain.

But the wound still rankles. I repeat that it is absolutely true that *I could have won*. The girl's name was May Coggeshall. She lived in Bayswater. There – that ought to convince you.

Waiting

James Reeves

Waiting, waiting, waiting
    For the party to begin;
Waiting, waiting, waiting
    For the laughter and din;
Waiting, waiting, waiting
    With hair just so
And clothes trim and tidy
    From top-knot to toe.
The floor is all shiny,
    The lights are ablaze;
There are sweetmeats in plenty
    And cakes beyond praise.
Oh the games and dancing,
    The tricks and the toys,
The music and the madness
    The colour and noise!
Waiting, waiting, waiting
    For the first knock on the door –
Was ever such waiting,
    Such waiting before?

World Without End

Helen Thomas

War changes everything, even Christmas. In December 1916 many men were away from home, and Helen Thomas received news that her writer husband, Edward, serving with the Artists' Rifles, was not granted Christmas leave.

'Christmas must be prepared for, however,' I thought, and I became busy with cakes and puddings and what I could afford of Christmas fare, which was little enough. The children with me planned the box I should pack for Edward, with something of everything, including crackers and sweets, and they began to make their presents for him. Into these preparations which before had always gone with such happy zest the same feeling of unreality entered and my eagerness was assumed for the sake of the children. But they too found it difficult to anticipate with joy a Christmas so strange, and the activities fell flat. Outside circumstances mattered as never before – our poverty, the severity of the weather, the dreariness of the house – and over us all an indefinable shadow fell.

But a miracle happened. Suddenly this Christmas of all Christmasses became the most joyous; the snow-bound forest sparkled like Aladdin's Cave; the house was transformed into a festive bower of holly and ivy and fir boughs, and our listlessness was changed into animated happiness and excitement.

Edward after all *was* coming home for Christmas!

The letter telling me this arrived by the first post along with one in a strange hand which I opened first, little suspecting what news Edward's contained. Inside this letter was a cheque for £20 made out to me and signed by the name of a writer of distinction whom I did not know. I stared and stared, and fumbling in the envelope for some explanation found a note

from Eleanor [Farjeon] telling me that she had been asked to forward this to me as a gift from a private fund. What could I not do with £20! I had never had so much in my life. But oh, if only Edward had been coming home!

Seeing his letter, which in my bewilderment I had forgotten, I read only the first words: 'My dearest, my draft leave will include Christmas after all!' I raced upstairs to the sleeping children. 'Wake up, wake up! Daddy is coming home for Christmas. He's coming home. He'll be here tomorrow, and I've got £20 to spend, and we'll all have the most wonderful presents; and oh, he's coming home.' Half-crying and half-laughing I lifted the children out of bed, and we danced in a ring and sang 'He's coming home for Christmas' to the tune of 'For he's a jolly good fellow'.

How we worked that day to get all ready! I snatched a couple of hours to go to London and do the shopping. I bought for Edward the best Jaeger sleeping-bag and thick gauntlet gloves and a volume of Shakespeare's sonnets, and for the children a real magic lantern with moving slides, and a special present for each one. I brought fruit and sweets and luxuries we had never tasted before, and wine as well. A frock of Edward's favourite red was my present to myself, and secretly for Myfanwy the children and I dug a little Christmas tree out of the garden and loaded it with toys and trinkets, and candles ready to light.

'Tomorrow is Christmas Day,' they kept saying. 'Tomorrow is Christmas Day.' In the midst of all this happy activity and looking forward, that word 'tomorrow' struck a note I could not help hearing, but I would not let it mean anything to me then. Tomorrow and tomorrow and tomorrow – the word was trying to shatter the joy of my soul with its knell-like reverberations.

'Today Daddy is coming home. Soon he'll be here, and after you've been to sleep you'll wake up and today will be

Christmas Day,' I said. 'Don't talk of tomorrow when today is here and is so lovely.'

'Don't you want Christmas to come then, Mummy?'

'Yes, but I think today is nicer than tomorrow.'

'I see what Mother means,' Merfyn said, 'now that the war's on, some tomorrows are bound to be sad for lots of people, and *she* doesn't want to think of them, do you, Mummy?'

'Yes, it's a bit like that. But look at the clock. If you don't hurry, today will pay you out and vanish before you've met Daddy.'

Merfyn and Bronwen were soon ready to go to the bottom of the hill at the cross-roads about a mile from the house, where they were to meet Edward. Myfanwy and I stayed behind to toast the crumpets and boil the kettle.

'I wonder if I ever shall see a real Christmas-tree like the one Bronwen told me about that she had at school with toys and candles,' said Myfanwy with a sigh, reminded of the subject by rows of fir trees still growing in the nursery garden.

'Oh my darling, you shall have everything you ever dreamt of this Christmas.' And I catch her up in my arms, and she throws her arms round my neck. While I stand thus the air is cut with Edward's clear voice calling the old familiar coo-ee; then the sound of voices; then of heavy snow-clogged footsteps; then Edward at the door. He is here. He is home.

It was to be Edward Thomas's last Christmas: he died, in France,
in 1917.

The Holly on the Wall

W.H. *Davies*

Play, little children, one and all,
For holly, holly on the wall.
You do not know that millions are
This moment in a deadly war,
Millions of men whose Christmas bells
Are guns' reports and busting shells,
Whose holly berries, made of lead,
Take human blood to stain them red;
Whose leaves are swords, and bayonets too,
To pierce their fellow-mortals through.
For now the war is here, and men –
Like cats that stretch their bodies when
The light has gone and darkness comes –
Have armed and left their peaceful homes:
But men will be, when there's no war,
As gentle as you children are.
Play, little children, one and all,
For holly, holly on the wall.

Let's talk about XMAS FOOD

There won't be turkey on many tables this year; but the Christmas atmosphere will be there and the children's eyes will sparkle at simple treats, served gaily. From what we know of you, you'll make your Christmas catering a grand success in spite of difficulties, and we're out to help you all we can. Here are a few suggestions of general interest from letters we have sent to correspondents. A Happy Christmas to you!

When the Second World War began in 1939 young children were mostly concerned with such deprivations as sweet rationing. I caught snatches of the adults' conversation and thought, from what I heard, that there would be no more treats or parties. But I was wrong, and parents tried to make the most of those dark days.

78

The author wearing a party hat, 1940.

The Children's Party

Eiluned Lewis

Quick as shuttles the children move
  Through the lighted room,
Where flowers glow in the scented air
  And candles bloom;
Their voices are fresh as a field of larks
  Over springing wheat;
They weave the web of what is to come
  With their dancing feet.

Like eager ponies snuffing the grass
  And the south-west weather,
Tossing their heads and lifting their feet
  They run together.
By the purring fire on his nurse's knee
  The youngest one
Stretches his toes and his tiny hands
  To catch the fun.

Out in the night, over the snow,
Grimly the dark gun-carriages go,
Where are they bound for?
No one knows,
But the curtain shakes,
Oh, draw it close!

from How We Lived Then

Norman Longmate

In this treasure-chest of Second World War memories, Norman Longmate
includes the following two for Christmas 1941. The first from the War Diary
of a ten-year-old girl, the second from a Liverpool housewife.

I woke early, my brother was asleep, so I made sure the
blackout curtains were over the windows, and with my torch I
had a little peep at my presents. I had a pair of slacks (Mummy
made them out of a blanket, a paint-book, a pencil-box, and a
very nice handkerchief, a book of poetry from Mummy, a bar
of chocolate, a whole orange.

I have a very nice present for Mummy, I made it myself, a
kettle-holder. And a present for Daddy, I made it, it is a case

with needles and cottons and buttons in, so when he goes away he can sew his buttons on. I also made him a shoe-polisher. We had a lovely breakfast, fried bread and a nice egg. We're both very lucky, Richard and me, because Mummy and Daddy don't care much for eggs, or sweets.

My daughter had asked Father Christmas for a doll's house. We looked at each other in dismay. Then my brother found an old bird-cage. During the raids he worked on it; found bits of cardboard for the walls. The office waste-paper basket provided an old file which made the roof. He painted the floors. We hunted for all kinds of bits and pieces and a miracle was achieved . . . a piece of hessian, dyed red, fringed, made an elegant carpet. Never will I forget her face that dark Christmas morning and her childish voice piping 'There'll be bluebirds over the white cliffs of Dover' as she saw those tables and chairs, tiny pictures made from cigarette cards, her cries of joy as she discovered each new thing.

Cards and Carols

*My brother, sister and I waited eagerly for cards from our father, out in
France in the Army Intelligence Corps. We thought the ones in French very
superior and between us collected the entire story of Snow White.*

Nᵒ 1 Du haut du balcon, Blanche-Neige jette
une rose, au prince Charmant.

Reviens vite, il serait si doux
de partager avec toi !
Come home soon, I shall be so happy
to share it with you!

THÉ
BENOIT

My dear ANNE
    THANK YOU VERY
MUCH FOR YOUR LOVELY
XMAS CARd WHICH
ARRIVED ON CHRISTMAS
EVE. DId YOU pAINT
ITYOURSELF? I Hope
THE CABARET WAS A
SUCCESS ANd THAT YOU
ALL HAd a good TIME
AM GLAD YOU LIKE
THE BOOKS. DId YOU
HAVE SOME NICE
XMAS pRESENTS? I HAd
QUITE A good TIME BUT
IT WASNT LIKE BEING
AT HOME. PERHAps
NEXT YEAR.
        Love Kisses
            DAddy
            XXXX

from A Nursery in the Nineties

Eleanor Farjeon

Christmas cards arrive in shop windows before we arrive home from our summer holidays. The card industry has grown hugely since the first card was printed in 1843. It doesn't always fill us with joy and goodwill to read, as early as November, that a distant friend wishes us, 'Plenty of good food and cheer/At this jolly time of year.'
Here is Eleanor Farjeon's experience in 1902.

At Christmas now 'The Cremers' meant cards only. But they were always the *first* Christmas-Cards we received – dear little robins perched on babies' cradles, dear little girls in bonnets, with bunches of holly, 'To dear little Harry – dearl little Nelly – dear little Joe – dear little Bertie – with love from the Misses Cremer.' They came like heralds, early in December, when Christmas was three endless weeks away. Mother's voice calling: 'The Cremers' Cards have come!' brought us running. We looked, and knew that Christmas was coming too.

But posts are so uncertain, and Thanet and London not *quite* next-door, you know, and it would be dreadful to a pair of fond, remembering spinsters should their cards ever arrive a trifle late. To make quite sure, they began to despatch their Christmas-cards in November.

'Children! the Cremers' Christmas-cards!'

'Already?'

Christmas is not yet due for a full month. We run to collect the precious firstlings.

And years pass, you grow older, the things to be done, the occasions to prepare for, press a little more irksomely each year on ladies who, if they cannot still send cases of toys to little

Harry, Nellie, Joe, and Bertie, must *never* disappoint dear children of their Christmas Greetings.

'The Cremers' cards!' calls Mama, somewhere about Guy Fawkes' Day.

We return, one September, from the summer holiday. The golden weeks beside the sea have waned, but London streets are sunny, it is weeks yet to the time of fog, and fires.

Laughing too much to speak, she appears waving an envelope. '*No!*' exclaims Harry. But there they are, the Cremers' cards have come. 'To dear little Harry – dear little Nelly – dear little Joe and dear little Bertie —' The robins, and the little girls in bonnets.

Two of us at least are over twenty, and to-morrow it will be October the First.

That was the last of the Cremers' Christmas-cards. Then time went back on them.

from Drawn from Memory

E.H. Shepard

E.H. Shepard reveals a familiar situation in his autobiography:

I had sent off my Christmas cards: not many, but each of the Aunts had to have one; then of course Father and Mother (these were put by till tomorrow); and there were Gussie and Lizzie and her sisters. It was fortunate that I did not have to buy all these cards with my own meagre savings. Mother always kept such of last year's cards as had no writing on them, or only in pencil, and we were able to use these again. The pencil marks were erased, usually quite ineffectually, with a rather grubby piece of india-rubber, and a greeting written on top, heavily, and in ink, to help in the disguise. The procedure was fraught with dangers and I was only saved from disaster by Mother looking over my shoulder and saying, 'Darling, you *can't* send that one to Aunt Alicia. It's the one she sent me last year.'

In a little book of Recitations for Small Children, *undated, but with a feeling of pre-1920s, each poem is accompanied by careful and rather coy instructions for the performer. Among them was:*

A Little Christmas Card

Anon

This little Christmas card has come,
　　With greetings glad and gay,
To wish you all, both great and small,
　　A merry Christmas Day.

Then when the festive day is past
　　I'll just turn round, you see,
And wish you here a bright New Year,
　　Quite full of mirth and glee.

And last your little Christmas card
　　Will turn once more like this;
With smile so shy I'll say 'Good-bye,'
　　And throw you each a kiss.

For a very tiny girl. She should wear two cards hung round her neck on a ribbon, one at the back and the other in front. The front card should bear the words, 'A Merry Christmas,' either in print or in large and clear writing. The back card should say, 'A Happy New Year.' 'Glad' or 'bright' would do instead, if preferred. 1 Wave hand forward at the word 'all,' then raise hand high at word 'great,' and lower it nearly to the ground at the word 'small.' 2 Hold card in one hand and point with the other hand to the words on the card. 3 Turn slowly round so that the back card can be read easily. Remain with back to the audience, but head sideways, so that the words can be heard, while you say the third and fourth lines of verse. 4 Turn round once more to the front, holding the front card well in view. 5 Smile and kiss hand gracefully to audience.

A Little Christmas Card.

In sharp contrast, Edwin Morgan's poem is a reminder that nowadays many cards are made on the computer.

The Computer's First Christmas Card

Edwin Morgan

jollymerry
hollyberry
jollyberry
merryholly
happyjolly

jollyjelly

jellybelly

berrymerry

hollyheppy

jollyMolly

merryJerry

merryHarry

hoppyBarry

heppyJarry

boppyheppy

berryjorry

jorryjolly

moppyjelly

Mollymerry

Jerryjolly

bellyboppy

jorryhoppy

hollymoppy

Barrymerry

Jarryheppy

happyboppy

boppyjolly

jollymerry

merrymerry

merrymerry

merryChris

ammerryasa

Chrismerry

asMERRYCHR

YSANTHEMUM

I well remember the Christmas of 1962. We moved house the week before Christmas and it was snowing. My two-year-old son threw snowballs at his baby sister, confined to her push-chair, and I was taken back to the snowy days of my own childhood. when I would whine to be allowed out to make a snowman, until my mother cocooned me fatly in hood, scarf and wellingtons. The novelty quickly wore thin, and I was soon crying to come in from the cold. The snowman still features on Christmas cards and in books and poems, even though there is much less snow about.

The Snow-Man

Walter de la Mare

What shape is this in cowl of snow?
  Stiff broom and icy hat?
A saffron moon, half-hidden, stares –
  But what is she staring *at?*

The knocker dangles on the door,
  But stark as tree and post
He blankly eyes the bright green paint,
  Is silent as a ghost.

But wait till belfry midnight strike,
  And up to the stars is tossed
Shrill cockcrow! – *then*, he'll gadding go –
  And, at his heels, Jack Frost:

Broom over shoulder, away he'll go,
Finger-tips tingling, nose aglow,
Dancing and yodelling through the snow,
  And, at his heels, Jack Frost!

"What shape is this in cowl of snow?", illustration by Harold Jones.

The Man They Made

Hamish Hendry

We made a Man all by ourselves;
    We made him jolly fat;
We stuck a Pipe into his face,
    And on his head a Hat.

We made him stand upon one Leg,
    That so he might not walk;
We made his Mouth without a Tongue ,
    That so he might not talk.

We left him grinning on the Lawn
    That we to Bed might go;
But in the night he ran away –
    Leaving a heap of Snow!

In 1962 Virginia Graham, writing for Punch, *offered hope to all adults who found 'Christmas grows heavy with the years' when she added:*

Yet there is a moment, one brief
strange moment every year,
when the season's first carol is sung
and you hear it. There,
captured in notes, is the magic
the wonder, the beauty, the bright
white soul of the matter;
and you stand, mouth open,
your hand, perhaps on a pate de fois gras,
and all the loveliness you knew as a child,
and your dead dead innocence
come back into Christmas.

The Children's Carol

Eleanor Farjeon

Here we come again, again, and here we come again!
Christmas is a single pearl swinging on a chain,
Christmas is a single flower in a barren wood,
Christmas is a single sail on the salty flood,
Christmas is a single star in the empty sky,
Christmas is a single song sung for charity.
Here we come again, again, to sing to you again,
Give a single penny that we may not sing in vain.

Music by Denis Rice for Eleanor Farjeon's
poem, In the Week when Christmas Comes.

from A Testament of Friendship

Vera Brittain

*Winifred Holtby had written of a childhood memory in an article called
'Harking back to long ago', and her great friend, Vera Brittain recaptured this
in her 1940 memoir.*

Winifred and Grace, aged four and six-and-a-half, lay awake on
Christmas Eve gazing through the square uncurtained window
at the frosty constellations of winter stars. The maids clattering
in the pantry below them had at last become silent; only the
occasional clank of an iron-shod hoof in the horse-pasture
broke the stillness of the night – when suddenly came the
crunch of feet on the gravel of the drive, the soft flicker of the
lantern and the joyous tumult of a Christmas carol. In a second
the two small girls were out of bed, scampering barefoot along
the nursery passage, up two steps into a terrifying stretch of
unlighted corridor, past the silver cupboard that harboured

Cover of the *Ladybird Book of Christmas Customs*, 1964.

ghosts and tigers, on to the front landing, and through a door into the best spare bedroom.

Peering between the slats of the venetian blind, they saw the singers with pale faces and long black coats, standing in the moonlight and starlight and lantern-light and lamplight streaming from the drawing-room window on the semi-circular sweep of the gravel. The chill draught blowing through the cold bedroom was sharp as icy water on the children's shivering bodies; they gathered their nightdresses round them and huddled ecstatically together for warmth as the twenty men and boys from the church choir went on singing round the schoolmaster's lantern. 'I can close my eyes and see them,' Winifred Holtby wrote a quarter of a century later. 'I can shut my ears and hear them; in the warmth of my lighted room I can feel the wind on my bare arms, and the chill boards under my naked feet. I can even smell the queer, cold, frosty smell of the

unused bedroom. It is all there.

'But it is all mine. Nobody else can ever hear it as I heard and hear it. . . . When I die, nobody will ever again know that particular sweet, fierce exaltation which stirred the rapturous, unblurred imagination of a child.'

Christmas Day

Washington Irving

While I lay musing on my pillow, I heard the sound of little feet pattering outside of the door, and a whispering consultation. Presently a choir of small voices chanted forth an old Christmas carol, the burden of which was –

Rejoice, our Saviour he was born
On Christmas day in the morning.

I rose softly, slipped on my clothes, opened the door suddenly, and beheld one of the most beautiful little fairy groups that a painter could imagine. It consisted of a boy and two girls, the eldest not more than six, and lovely as seraphs. They were going the rounds of the house, and singing at every chamber door; but my sudden appearance frightened them into mute bashfulness. They remained for a moment playing on their lips with their fingers, and now and then stealing a shy glance, from under their eyebrows, until, as if by one impulse, they scampered away, and as they turned an angle of the gallery, I heard them laughing in triumph at their escape.

WISHING ⁑ YOU ⁑ A ⁑ HAPPY ⁑ CHRISTMAS ⁑

Perhaps these three children, 'lovely as seraphs', in the extract from Washington Irving's 1820 Christmas Day *above are a contrast to the naughty ones in Kit Wright's twentieth-century poem.*

The Wicked Singers
Kit Wright

And have you been out carol singing,
Collecting for the Old Folk's Dinner?

Oh yes indeed, oh yes indeed.

And did you sing all the Christmas numbers,
Every one a winner?
Oh yes indeed, oh yes indeed.

Good King Wenceslas, and Hark
The Herald Angels Sing?

Oh yes indeed, oh yes indeed.

And did you sing them loud and clear
And make the night sky ring?

Oh yes indeed, oh yes indeed.

And did you count up all the money?
Was it quite a lot?

Oh yes indeed, oh yes indeed.

And did you give it all to the Vicar,
Everything you'd got?

Certainly not, certainly not.

Alexander Martin was fourteen when he wrote this piece for the 1971
Children's Annual, Allsorts, *recalling his time at Winchester Choir School.*

The Year I was 8: A Christmas Choirtime

Alexander Martin

It was the last day of my first term and everybody was getting ready to go home; everybody? No: the choristers had to stay behind until Christmas. After all, there must be a Christmas Service and a Carol Service. Poor things, you may say. But it's quite fun really. There are no lessons, just two hours of practice every day, and the service in the Cathedral in the evening.

There are twenty choristers, and twenty is an ideal number of people to live in a school designed for a hundred. We could play no end of outdoor games, there was our own set of Scalextric racing cars, we could swim in the pool, and expeditions were arranged to various places.

As Christmas came on, the Carol Service was sung in the Cathedral. We sang many well-known carols with the congregation, and a few not so well-known ones by ourselves. Most of the service was lit only with candles and lanterns, which made it quite exciting, and a huge Christmas tree was put up in the Cathedral, reaching almost to the roof. About two thousand people came to the service, and it truly was a great occasion.

However, when it was all over, after three long processions around the Cathedral, it was about ten o'clock and I was terribly tired.

On Christmas Day we got presents from each member of the staff. We got up and had an extra large breakfast. Then we had an extra large practice for three extra large services. The first service was the Nativity Service in the morning, with the Crib. Many people came to this service, and we mainly sang carols. The highlight of the service came when everybody processed up the nave to the place where the Crib was, near the altar. The Crib itself had a real manger with real hay and straw, and life-sized figures in it. After the Nativity Service there was Holy Communion, when grown-ups take the bread and wine, and children can go to the altar rail although they won't have any bread or wine.

After that service we all had Christmas dinner. There were two huge turkeys which looked as if they'd just come out of *Gulliver's Travels*. We each had an enormous helping, with tons of stuffing, gallons of bread sauce and galaxies of brussels sprouts. After the dinner we had to pack our things and clear up the School. Then we had another long practice for the last service of the term. This was really a glorified Evensong with the Psalms, Magnificat and Nunc Dimittis, but there was a long procession and carols as well.

The Nativity

*For many, the religious side of Christmas is the most meaningful, and the
Nativity the highlight of the church and school year.*

Carol

John Short

There was a Boy bedded in bracken,
Like to a sleeping snake all curled he lay;
On his thin navel turned this spinning sphere,
Each feeble finger fetched seven suns away.
He was not dropped in good-for-lambing weather,
He took no suck when shook buds sing together,
But he is come in cold-as-workhouse weather,
Poor as a Salford child.

*One Sunday School production I directed stands out in my memory. At the
Dress Rehearsal the shepherds, with towels around their heads, wearing
dressing gowns and holding home-made crooks, waited expectantly. The
kings, their cardboard crowns adorned with fruit gums for jewels, were also
in position. The Angel Gabriel, a blond ballet dancer, practised her pirouettes
down the aisle of the rather austere Ealing Abbey (quite unscripted!) and
Mary and Joseph slowly made their way to the Stable.*

MARY: I'm so tired, Joseph . . . I must rest a while.
JOSEPH: (kindly) Well, lean on me, Mary.
          (Mary leans heavily on Joseph. Joseph, indignantly

moves away. Mary rolls down the Altar steps and bursts into tears)

ME: (not kindly): JOSEPH! What was all that about?

JOSEPH: It's only the Dress Rehearsal. She shouldn't lean on me at the Dress Rehearsal. She can lean on me tomorrow.

And she did, and all went splendidly next day. A nun, visiting from Italy, had tears in her eyes, and said she would never forget the true tenderness between Joseph and Mary, the shepherds, kings, and Gabriel ('He seemed to almost dance. . . !') or the small boy who sang:

Shepherd boys are two a penny
And no treasures I bring
Will he look at me? Will he
notice me?
I can only sing . . .

As the proud mother of both singing shepherd and Mary (and very fond of Joseph, who lived a few doors from us) I positively glowed, unlike the nursery school teacher whose infants were allowed to improvise their own dialogue and brought the house down with:

MARY (aged 4) Oh there you are, Joseph! 'Ere, take 'im for a bit so I can put me feet up. He's been a right little bugger all day!

Jesus' Christmas Party

This popular nativity story by Nicholas Allan can also be enjoyed in a delightful picture book version, and as a play.

There was nothing the innkeeper liked more than a good night's sleep.

But that night there was a knock at the door.

'No room', said the innkeeper.

'But we're tired and have travelled through night and day.'

'There's only one stable round the back. Here's two blankets. Sign the register.'

So they signed it: 'Mary and Joseph'.

Then he shut the door, climbed the stairs, got into bed, and went to sleep.

But then, later, there was another knock at the door.

'Excuse me. I wonder if you could lend us another, smaller, blanket?'

'There. One smaller blanket,' said the innkeeper.

Then he shut the door, climbed the stairs, got into bed, and went to sleep.

But then a bright light woke him up.

'That's ALL I need,' said the inn-keeper.

Then he shut the door, climbed the stairs, drew the curtains, got into bed, and went to sleep.

But then there was ANOTHER knock at the door.

'We are three shepherds.'

'Well, what's the matter? Lost your sheep?'

'We've come to see Mary and Joseph.'

'ROUND THE BACK', said the innkeeper.

Then he shut the door, climbed the stairs, got into bed, and went to sleep.

But then there was yet ANOTHER knock at the door.

'We are three kings. We've come . . . '

'ROUND THE BACK!'

He slammed the door, climbed the stairs, got into bed, and went to sleep.

But THEN a chorus of singing woke him up.

'RIGHT – THAT DOES IT!'

So he got out of bed, stomped down the stairs, threw open the door, went round the back, stormed into the stable, and was just about to speak when –

'Ssshh!' whispered everybody, 'you'll wake the baby!'

'BABY?' said the innkeeper.

'Yes, a baby has this night been born.'

'Oh?' said the innkeeper, looking crossly into the manger.

And just at that moment, suddenly, amazingly, his anger seemed to fly away.

'Oh,' said the innkeeper, 'isn't he LOVELY!'

In fact, he thought he was so special, he woke up ALL the guests at the inn, so they could come and have a look at the baby too. So no one got much sleep that night.

A Christmas Verse

Anon

He had not royal palace,
Only a stable bare.
    He had no watchful servants,
An ox and ass stood there.
But light shone forth from where He lay;
The King of Love upon the hay!

Baa, Baa, Black sheep

'Baa, Baa, black sheep
Have you any wool?'
'Yes sir, yes sir, three bags full,
One for the old man
And one for the Maid,
And one for the little Boy
That's in the manger laid.'

from Peepshow

Marguerite Steen

*I'm in favour of children putting on their own entertainments, as a change
from watching television or playing computer games. In this 1933 book the
author pretended to be Angela, second child in the Borthwick family, who
acted plays at home.*

Sometimes we act a short Christmas play – it depends whether
we have time to get one ready; because, as you know, one only

has a few days between breaking up and Christmas, and what with buying presents and all the hullabaloo of getting Christmas ready, not to mention parties and such like, there isn't much time for proper rehearsals.

And last Christmas we found a beauty: it is by Herbert and Eleanor Farjeon, and is called *A Room at the Inn*.

We found it in the 1931 *Radio Times Christmas Number* – too late, worse luck, to produce it in time for last Christmas, but we are going to do it this year, and Selina has made up the most darling little tune for the opening chorus:

> Birds in the air,
> Beasts in the byre,
> Straw for thy bed,
> Stars for thy fire.

I expect you could get this quite easily if you wrote to the *Radio Times* for it, or, if not, I expect the Farjeons will be publishing it in one of their books of poetry sooner or later. Anyhow, there are parts for the Ox and the Ass; for the Host and Hostess of the Inn and two Servants; and there are Joseph and Mary, and a great tumult of noises off.

Nigel is arranging the production, and he is going to have the stage cut into two parts, half for the Stable and half for the Inn, and in front shall be the street along which Joseph and Mary arrive, asking for room at the Inn; and the Ox and the Ass shall just show their heads over a partition at the back of the Stable. Of course, we have the animal heads already – they are beauties, which Uncle Bim got us from Clarkson's.

As today you won't be able to get the play from the Radio Times, *here is the opening scene, between the Ox and the Ass.*

106

from A Room at the Inn

Herbert and Eleanor Farjeon

Angelic Voices
Birds in the air,
Beasts in the byre,
Straw for thy bed,
Stars for thy fire,
Thy Body for bread,
Thy Blood for the wine,
A thorn for thy crown,
A cross for thy sign.

In the stable: the ASS brays. The OX lows.

OX: Come in, brother Ass, come in, can't ye, without making that rumpus?

ASS: We're with the voices we're born with, brother Ox. If I'd been born with a nightingale's tongue, I'd come in like a nightingale. Being born with a bray, I comes in like an ass.

OX: Where have you been this bitter night?

ASS: Watching of the doings at the Inn. There's company expected.

OX: What company?

ASS: Grand company, by the looks of it. Lights in the hall! Bustle in the bedchambers! Clatter in the kitchens! The larder's full of fodder and swill. They're garnishing the feast-rooms. There'll be lords on stallions and ladies on gennets. Oh, brother!

OX: Well then?

ASS: D'ye think they'll stall the grand horses along of us in the stable here?

OX: Along of us? You're ambitious, you are! You think high, you do! What! Thoroughbreds lie in *our* dung? None but the meanest'll grace this place tonight.

ASS: None but the meanest?

OX: Ay—that's you and me.

ASS: And lucky if it's you, brother Ox!

I seed a roasting-spit in the kitchen 'ld take your carcase whole.

OX: You don't scare me, brother Ass. If I'd been to be roasted tonight, I'd ha' been slaughtered last week. Well hung, they likes their roast, they gentry does.

> *They sing*
> We draws their loads,
> We bears their packs,
> We feels their whips,
> Upon our backs;
> They eats our flesh,
> They tans our hides,
> So they consumes
> What we provides.

OX: In my tough skin
Their feet they warm—

ASS: In my rough pell
They fear no storm—

BOTH: And when we dies
They make no fuss,
For what's to them
The likes of us?

The Friendly Beasts

Traditional

Jesus, our brother, kind and good,
Was humbly born in a stable rude,
And the friendly beasts around Him stood;
Jesus, our brother, kind and good.

'I,' said the donkey, shaggy and brown,
'I carried His mother up hill and down;
I carried her safely to Bethlehem town;
I,' said the donkey, shaggy and brown.

'I,' said the dove from the rafters high,
'Cooed Him to sleep, that He should not cry,
We cooed Him to sleep, my mate and I.
'I,' said the dove from the rafters high.

'I,' said the cow, all white and red,
'I gave Him my manger for His bed;
I gave Him my hay to pillow His head;
I,' said the cow, all white and red.

'I,' said the sheep with curly horn,
'I gave Him my wool for His blanket warm.
He wore my coat on Christmas morn.
I,' said the sheep with curly horn.

Thus every beast by some good spell,
In the stable dark was glad to tell
Of the gift he gave Emmanuel,
The gift he gave Emmanuel.

Christmas Night

Anon

Softly, softly, through the darkness
  Snow is falling.
Sharply, sharply, in the meadows
  Lambs are calling.
Coldly, coldly, all around me
  Winds are blowing.
Brightly, brightly, up above me
  Stars are glowing.

Nativity Lament

Jenny Owen

Christmas 1999 is one that Jennifer Owen will never forget. She was six then, and one of 350 pupils at Hilmarton Primary School in Calne, Wiltshire, who had entered a local competition. The aim was to write, in no more than fifty words, why he or she deserved to be chosen to turn on Calne's Christmas lights.

Jenny's entry went like this:

Because I'm never a fairy, an angel or Mary, a wise man, a shepherd or a King. But always a helper, a singer, an extra, and this year a grumpy old sheep. And this would make me feel really important.

The school play that year was *The Grumpy Sheep*, an alternative Nativity story. No one guessed that Jenny, always a quiet little girl, longed for a big part, until she expressed her feelings in writing. To her surprise and delight she won the competition, and on 3 December turned on the lights with the Mayor of Calne. But the story didn't end there. When it reached the national press, the Prime Minister's wife, Cherie Blair, invited Jenny to London to switch on the 120 white lights on the 18 ft tree, with its crystal snowflakes and doves, outside No 10 Downing Street.

'Nativity Lament Wins Jenny a Place in the Limelight' read one newspaper caption. Jenny herself commented, 'I was really excited. I had tickles in my tummy.' It was a real-life fairy story, a child's wish come true, and a Christmas to remember.

from 101 Dalmatians

Dodie Smith

*Once, on a night of stars and one especially large, bright star, nearly one 100
dalmatians in this much-loved story were on the run from danger, when they
came to a grey stone building with a tower at one end. They could just
squeeze through the narrow door:*

'No hay in this barn' said the Cadpig.

She had counted on the hay for warmth, but she soon found
she was warm enough without it, for there was a big stove
alight. It had a long iron pipe for a chimney which went right
up through the raftered ceiling. The moon was out again now
and its light was streaming in through the tall windows, so that
the clear glass made silver patterns on the stone floor and the
coloured glass made blue, gold and rose patterns. The Cadpig
patted one of the coloured patterns with a delicate paw.

'I love this barn,' she said.

Patch said: 'I don't think it *is* a barn.' But he liked it as much as the Cadpig did.

They wandered around – and suddenly they made a discovery. Whatever this mysterious place was, it was certainly intended for puppies. For in front of every seat – and there were many seats – was a puppy-sized dogbed, padded and most comfortable.

'Why, it's just *meant* for us all to sleep in!' said the Cadpig.

'I'll tell the other pups,' said Patch, starting for the door. A glad cry from the Cadpig called him back.

'Look, look! Television!'

But it was not like the Television at Hell Hall. It was much larger. And the figures on the screen did not move or speak. Indeed, it was not a screen. The figures were really there, on a low platform, humans and animals, most life-like, though smaller than in real life. They were in a stable, above which was one bright star.

'Look at the little humans, kneeling,' said Patch.

'And there's a kind of a cow,' said the Cadpig, remembering the cows at the farm, who had given all the pups milk.

'And a kind of a horse,' said Patch, remembering the helpful horse who had let them all out of the field.

'No dogs,' said the Cadpig. 'What a pity! But I like it much better than ordinary Television. Only I don't know why.'

Then they heard Lucky and the others, who had found their way in. Soon every pup was curled up on a comfortable dogbed and fast asleep – except the Cadpig. She had dragged along one of the dogbeds by its most convenient little carpet ear, and was sitting on it, wide awake, gazing and gazing at this new and far more beautiful Television.

Trees and Trimmings

Christmas trees are one of the most special and magical of all Christmas symbols. The present tradition began during the reign of Queen Victoria, who once wrote that the tree ceremony 'quite affected our dear Albert who turned pale and had tears in his eyes and pressed my hand, very warmly. . .'.

Advice to a Child

Eleanor Farjeon

Set your fir-tree
In a pot;
Needles green
Is all it's got.
Shut the door
And go away,
And so to sleep
Till Christmas Day.
In the morning
Seek your tree,
And you shall see
What you shall see.

from Days at Wickham

Anne Viccars Barber

Christmas! How lovely it is. Early in the morning we open our stockings. Up till now I have believed in Father Christmas but something has made me doubt his existence. In my stocking were some tiny clothes pegs for my dolls and when Mary saw them she said '*Those* came from my school bazaar.' After breakfast we go to church and remember it is the birthday of Jesus. At lunch there is turkey and plum pudding. Nanny brings in the Christmas pudding with dancing flames round it. It reminds me of a dragon breathing fire. After tea we gather round the Christmas tree for our presents. The tree glows with lighted candles. It is a beautiful moment. Time seems to stand still.

The Song of the Christmas Tree Fairy

Cicely M. Barker

The little Christmas Tree was born
And dwelt in open air;
It did not guess how bright a dress
Some day its boughs would wear;
Brown cones were all, it thought, a tall
And grown-up Fir would bear.

O little Fir! Your forest home
Is far and far away;
And here indoors these boughs of yours
With coloured balls are gay,

With candle-light, and tinsel bright,
For this is Christmas Day!

A dolly-fairy stands on top,
Till children sleep; then she
(A live one now!) from bough to bough
Goes gliding silently.
O magic sight, this joyous night!
O laden, sparkling tree!

from The Only Child

James Kircup

We had a tiny, artificial Christmas tree that stood in a white-painted wooden base made to represent a tub. The branches of the tree were of stiff wire covered with green thread and paper pine needles; each branch had a very realistic tip of lighter green, with an orange berry on the end. When the Christmas tree was brought out and unwrapped from last year's newspapers, there was the delight of pulling the folded-up branches into place, bending each one slightly, so that the tip pointed upwards. Then we would hang it with bright baubles and tinsel and stars and shimmering 'icicles,' and at the very top we clipped a brilliant blue bird with a spun-glass dome of birds and shells and flowers. There were holders for candles on the tree, too, and we put brightly-coloured candles in them. Unfortunately, as the tree was of paper, we could not light them, but I didn't mind – it was even more wonderful to imagine what the tree would look like if they were lit.

from The Country Child

Alison Uttley

A few days before Christmas Tom Garland and Dan took a bill-hook and knife and went into the woods to cut branches of scarlet-berried holly. They tied them together with ropes and dragged them down over the fields, to the barn. Tom cut a bough of mistletoe from the ancient hollow hawthorn which leaned over the wall by the orchard, and thick clumps of dark-berried ivy from the walls.

Indoors Mrs Garland and Susan and Becky polished and rubbed and cleaned the furniture and brasses, so that everything glowed and glittered. They decorated every room, from the kitchen where every lustre jug had its sprig in its mouth, every brass candlestick had its chaplet, every copper saucepan and preserving-pan had its wreath of shining berries and leaves, through the hall, which was a bower of green, to the two parlours which were festooned and hung with holly and boughs of fir, and ivy berries dipped in red raddle, left over from sheep marking.

Holly decked every picture and ornament. Sprays hung over the bacon and twisted round the hams and herb bunches. The clock carried a crown on his head, and every dish-cover had a little sprig. Susan kept an eye on the lonely forgotten humble things, the jelly moulds and colanders and nutmeg-graters, and made them happy with glossy leaves. Everything seemed to speak, to ask for its morsel of greenery, and she tried to leave out nothing.

Holly

Christina Rossetti

But give me holly, bold and jolly,
Honest, prickly, shining holly;
Pluck me holly leaf and berry
For the day when I make merry.

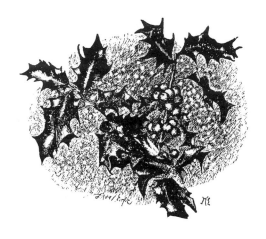

Poem For Allan

Robert Frost

*Robert Frost, American poet and New England farmer, was not pleased when
a stranger, a city type, asked if he would sell his Christmas trees. In his poem
'A Christmas Circular Letter' he writes of young fir balsams, saying, 'I hadn't
thought of them as Christmas trees.' Of course he refuses to sell. I
remembered the poem when I was going through a pile of the American
children's magazine* Cricket & Company *and came upon another Frost poem
in the 1974 issue. It was introduced as: '. . . an unpublished poem written by
Frost sixty years ago for Allan Neilson, an 8-year-old friend of his. The poet's
daughter, Lesley, drew the Christmas trees.*

For Allan
Who wanted to see how I wrote
a poem.

Among these mountains, do you know,
I have a farm, and on it grow
A thousand lovely Christmas trees.
I'd like to send you one of these,
But it's against the laws.
A man may give a little boy
A book, a useful knife, a toy,
Or even a rhyme like this by me
(I write it just like this you see).
But nobody may give a tree
Excepting Santa Claus.

Robert Frost

Emily Pepys' Journal

Emily Pepys, a collateral descendant of Samuel, kept a journal in 1845 when she was eleven and a quarter.

Tuesday, 24th December. In the morning a Mistletoe was brought into the schoolroom and in the afternoon some Holly was brought in which we made into the words 'Jolly Christmas', it was very difficult and we pricked out fingers a great deal. Herbert nailed it up and Emie and I shaped and cut it the right lengths: it was my thought and everybody admired it very much. I thought of 'Christmas' and Herbert thought of putting 'Jolly' before it. We made a wreath of laurels and put it on old Homer's head, that is on a bust of him: we had capital fun all the afternoon. We had a very jolly tea and altogether spent a very merry Christmas Eve. In the evening Papa read Pickwick to the great amusement of the Sullivans, and we sat up till half past ten as the servants were dancing.

Sadly, she noted next day
Wednesday, 25th December. A very melancholy beginning to Chrstmas Day as the house has been on fire . . .

Under the Mistletoe

Anon

With a sprig of mistletoe –
Grandmamma caught napping –
Master Dick doth softly go,
Hand on chair-back clapping.

'Steady, steady, now's the time
For a kiss, dear Granny;
When you wake it *will* be prime –
I love you best of any!'

from Little Kisses for Misses, 1880.

The Christmas Tree

John Walsh

They chopped her down in some far wood
A week ago,
Shook from her dark green spikes her load
Of gathered snow.
And brought her home at last, to be
Our Christmas snow.

A week she shone, sprinkled with lamps
And fairy frost:
Now, with her boughs all stripped, her lights
And spangles lost,
Out in the garden there, leaning
On a broken post.

She sighs gently . . . Can it be
She longs to go
Back to that far-off wood, where green
And wild things grow?
Back to her dark green sisters, standing
In wind and snow?

The Secret, illustration by Harold Jones.

124

Players and Pantomimes

*The tradition of mumming pre-dates our Christmas. The plays ususully
celebrate life over death, or good over evil, and different parts of the country
have their own versions. The 'actors' were rather like Shakespeare's 'rude
mechanicals' in* A Midsummer Night's Dream, *local tradespeople, craftsmen
and farm-workers out for a bit of fun and to make money for charity. Much
of the enjoyment came from raw, or over-dramatic, acting, with plenty of
audience participation. The characters varied, but often included St George
and his enemies, the Dragon and the fierce Turkish Knight. There was often a
Clown, or a Fool, Little Devil Doubt who swept the stage, and, from
Victorian days, a top-hatted Doctor who could cure, according to his own
boast:*

The itch, the stitch, the palsy and the gout,

Pains within and pains without;

If the devil were in I'd fetch him out!

And, as Master of Ceremonies, there was often Father Christmas.

Mummer's Song
Traditional

Now welcome, welcome Christmas
With a right good cheer
Away dumps, away dumps
Nor come you not here
And I wish you a merry Christmas
And a Happy New Year.

The Mummers
Eleanor Farjeon

Here's greeting for the master,
And for the mistress greeting,
And greeting for each gallant lad
And every pretty sweeting,
And greeting for the little children
Dancing round our meeting.

We be your servants all,
We be merry mummers;
We know jolly winter's face
Though we ne'er saw summer's;
We come in wi' the end o' the year,
For we be Christmas-comers.

This here do be Saint George,
This the heathen Paynim,
Dragon he will drink your healths
When Saint George has slain him;
This do be a beautiful maid,
And a trouble 'twere to train him!

There's our mumming ended
And nothing to distress ye –
Surely, we be little loth
Since so kindly press ye.
Here's God bless ye, master, mistress,
All the house, God bless ye!

The Wednesday Group in *St George and the Dragon*

When I ran a local drama class called The Wednesday Group for my children and their friends, St George and The Dragon was the highlight of the year. It opened with a lively parade down the street, the cast in costume, playing instruments, carrying lanterns and greenery, and arriving in our breakfast room where an audience of friends and family waited expectedly as little Devil Doubt introduced the event:

I open the door, I enter in,
I hope your favour we shall win.
My friends and I have come today
To act you all a merry play.
Whether we rise or whether we fall
We'll do our best to please you all.

THE CAST: We'll do our best to please you all . . .
DRAGON: O pardon, pardon, brave St George,
One thing I do implore

Grant me my life and I'll leave you
In peace for evermore.

ST GEORGE: No, no, that may not be,
For thus is the story told
Of how the brave St George
DID slay the Dragon bold. . . .

(They fight . . . the cast cheer loudly as St George slays the Dragon a second time . . . and little Devil Doubt sweeps him away)

DEVIL DOUBT: Room, room, for me and my broom. . . .

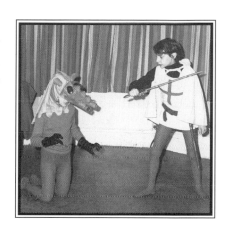

(The play closes with)

FATHER CHRISTMAS:
Ladies and Gentlemen, our sport is done
We can no longer stay,
Remember now, that evermore,
St George will win the day
Ladies and gentlemen, we dare to hope,
If you've enjoyed our play
That you will now give to our cause
As freely as you may. . . .

(It comes to an abrupt end . . . while audience gave money, the cast used to sing, 'We wish you a Merry Christmas' . . .)

Illustration by David Frankland commissioned by the Royal Shakespeare Company for its production of *The Lion, the Witch and the Wardrobe*.

U is for Uncle

Eleanor Farjeon

Uncle is the sort of man
Who comes at an unusual time,
And calls out 'Hullo, Kiddies! Can
You take me to the Pantomime?'

The play's no sooner over than
He bellows very heartily,
'Well what about it, Kiddies? Can
You manage ices for your tea?'

And without any previous plan,
When taking leave, as like as not,

He chinks his pockets shouting, 'Can
You spend Five Shillings, Kiddies, what?'

Uncle is that sort of man,
And as for Us, of course we can!

'Going to the Pantomime' by John Leech, *The Illustrated London News*,
24 December 1853.

*I don't know which I enjoyed more – being taken to the pantomime as a child
or playing in pantomime as an actress. Both had memorable moments, and
uneasy ones. I was never fond of the slap-stick sequence and it worried me to
see custard oozing down the comic's face. In* The Sleeping Beauty *there was a
moment I always dreaded. The Story Teller (top hat and frock coat) and the
Little Girl (me in pink pyjamas) not only kept the plot going with dialogue but
had to greet the children who came up on stage, hand out balloons (having
blown them up in the interval) and sing with them:*

Who put the dots on the Dalmatian dog,
How did he get that way?
Who put the dots on the Dalmatian dog . . .
Somebody's got to say.
Hi diddle ho!
I want to know.
The question has set me agog
Oh what shall I do,

First Time

Jan Dean

My dad's in the pantomime.
My dad is a star.
My dad's better than your dad
And funnier by far.
My dad tells the best jokes
My dad sings great songs
My dad's in the wings now
He's coming. Won't be long.

Cyril Fletcher was an eye-catching, eye-rolling, roguish and quite
unforgettable Dame in *The Sleeping Beauty* at the Hippodrome,
Norwich, in 1952.

My dad doesn't look right
My dad's not like that
He doesn't have long hair at home
That's not his proper hat.
He doesn't have big bright red lips
Or bosoms like balloons.
I want my dad back like he was.
I want to go home. Soon.

Why did no one tell me
That he'd be in disguise?
I think it's sort of scary;
I know they're my dad's eyes,
But who's the face they're peeping from?
And whose the painted grin?
Whose is the huge black beauty spot
Upon his powdered chin?
My dad's mixed up with other bits
Of people I don't know.
He's chopped and changed.
All rearranged. Down in the second row
I howl. My father's lost.

This pantomime's a monster,
Don't believe its jolly song.
The panto ate my father
Then spat him out all wrong.
I hate the bouncy dancers
Tap-tapping in a line.
This pantomime's pretending
Its smile is Frankenstein.

PINKIE & THE FAIRIES AT HIS MAJESTY'S THEATRE.

MASTER PHILIP TONGE AS TOMMY. MISS GWENNIE BROGDEN AS CINDERELLA. MISS IRIS HAWKINS AS PINKIE.

Once again "Pinkie and the Fairies" has been selected as the season's play for children at His Majesty's. The young folks are giving this delightful performance a right royal reception.

MR EDWARD TERRY AS UNCLE GREGORY.

BARONESS VON HUTTEN AS AUNT IMOGEN.

WHERE CHILDREN RULE.

MISS MARJORIE DANE AS QUEEN OF THE LAND WHERE CHILDREN RULE.

Children have an opportunity of seeing the land where they rule supreme at the Garrick. And a very delightful land it is, too. The youngsters have declared "Where Children Rule" a complete success.

MASTER BOBBIE ANDREWS AS DAVID PENNYFEATHER.

AT THE GARRICK THEATRE.

MISS STELLA TERRY AS ELIZABETH PENNYFEATHER.

from The Only Child

James Kircup

One of my earliest unpleasant memories is connected with Christmas. I must have been only about two years old at the time, because I remember being carried in my mother's arms into a theatre. 'Theatre' is really too noble a word for it: it was, I think, a large hall with a curtained platform at one end. The hall was near the sea, beside the blue-and-white lifeboat under its Moorish canopy, beside the Figure of Eight and the Mecca Tearooms and the tram terminus at the Wouldhave Memorial in Ocean Road. The matinée performance must have begun when we entered because we sat in pitch darkness near the back of the hall; I think the sudden darkness after the wave-lit brightness of Ocean Road may have contributed to my fright. It was a pantomime – *Jack and the Beanstalk* – that was offered to my startled gaze. I knew it was all perfectly horrible, yet I didn't know why. Then a line of chorus girls came on, in very brief red satin skirts and with huge floppy orange bows in their hair, and started kicking their legs in the air and shuffling and stamping their feet with hectic vigour. As they danced, they sang, with the vivacious, breathless flatness of third-rate hoofers. This was the crowning horror. I turned my head away and refused to look at the stage, and let out shriek after shriek of utter dismay and frightened fury. Nothing would quiet me. The girls went on and on, and so did I. Finally, my puzzled mother – 'I was *mad* with you,' she told me years later – carried me outside, still screaming as if all the chorus girls in hell were after me.

The Pantomime

Guy Boas

Regularly at Christmas-time
We're taken to the Pantomime;
We think it's childish, but we go
Because Papa enjoys it so.

December

Rose Fyleman

All the months go past
Each is like a guest;
December is the last,
December is the best.

Each has lovely things,
Each one is a friend,
But December brings
Christmas at the end.

Acknowledgements

I am most grateful to all publishers, trustees, writers and artists who have given permission for their work to be used in *When Christmas Comes*. I would like to thank the following for particular kindness and support: Nicholas Allan, Kate and James Anderson, Julian Barnes, Quentin Blake, Simon Brett, Katrina Burnett, Shirley Hughes, Anita Israel, Philip and Catherine Owen, Myfanwy Thomas, Colin West, Bee and Walter Wyeth and the staff of the Pitshanger Bookshop, not forgetting the unceasing cooperation of all at Sutton Publishing, especially Jaqueline Mitchell and my very patient editor, Elizabeth Stone.

Nicholas Allan, *Jesus' Christmas Party* (Hutchinson, 1991), copyright © Nicholas Allan, and reprinted with his permission. Anne Viccars Barber, *Days at Wickham* (Geoffrey Bles, 1966). Cicely Mary Barker, 'The Song of the Christmas Tree Fairy', poem and illustration from *Flower Fairies of the Winter*, copyright © The Estate of Cecily Mary Barker 1940, 1990, 2002, reproduced by permission of Frederick Warne & Co. Simon Brett, *How to be a Little Sod* (Orion Publishing Group Ltd, 1992), copyright © Simon Brett and reprinted by permission of the author and the publisher. Vera Brittain, *Testament of Friendship* (1940) is included with the permission of Vera Brittain's literary executors, Mark Bostridge and Rebecca Williams. Richmal Crompton, 'William's Christmas Eve' from *More William* (1922), reprinted by permission of A.P. Watt Ltd on behalf of Richmal Ashbee. W.H. Davies, 'The

Holly on the Wall' from *Collected Poems* (Jonathan Cape, 1934), reprinted with the permission of the Literary Estate of W.H. Davies. Jan Dean, 'First Time' from *Nearly Thirteen* (Blackie, 1994), copyright © Jan Dean, reprinted with the author's permission. Walter de la Mare, 'The Snowman' from *This Year, Next Year* (Faber, 1937) and *The Complete Poems of Walter de la Mare* (1969), reprinted by permission of the Literary Trustees of Walter de la Mare and the Society of Authors as their representative. Eleanor Farjeon, 'In the Week When Christmas Comes', 'For Them', 'The Children's Carol', 'The Mummer' from *Come Christmas* (Collins, 1927 and The Cyder Press, 2000); 'Advice to a Child' from *The Children's Bells* (Oxford, 1957); 'Christmas Stocking' from *Blackbird has Spoken* (Macmillan, 1999); 'Menu for a King' from *The New Book of Days* (Oxford, 1941); extracts from *A Nursery in the Nineties* (Oxford, 1935); 'U is for Uncle' from *The Town Child's Alphabet* (The Poetry Bookshop, 1924). Herbert Farjeon, conundrums for the magazine *The Humorist*, 'Is Musical Chairs Immoral' from *The Herbert Farjeon Omnibus*; Extract from *A Room at the Inn* by Eleanor and Herbert Farjeon. Robert Frost, 'For Allan' / 'Who Wanted to see how I wrote a Poem', © the Estate of Robert Lee Frost, reprinted with, the Estate's permission. Rose Fyleman, 'December' from *Gay Go Up* (Methuen, 1929), reprinted by permission of the Society of Authors as the Literary Representatives of the Estate of Rose Fyleman. Mick Gowar, 'Christmas Thank-you's' from *Swings and Roundabouts* (Collins, 1987), copyright © Mick Gowar c. 1981 and reprinted with his permission. Rose Henniker Heaton, 'The Perfect Stocking' from *The Perfect Christmas* 1932, reprinted by permission of Burke's Peerage. Elizabeth Jennings, 'Afterthought' from *The Secret Brother* (Macmillan, 1966), reprinted by permission of David Higham Associates.

from *Three Houses* (Hamish Hamilton, 1999), copyright © Angela Thirkell 1931. Helen Thomas, extract from *World Without End and Under Storm's Wing* (Carcanet Press, 1988), copyright © Myfanwy Thomas. Alison Uttley, two extracts from *The Country Child* (Faber, 1931 and Jane Nissen Books, 2001), permission granted by The Society of Authors as the Literary Representative of the Alison Uttley Literary Property Estate. John Walsh, 'The Christmas Tree' from *Poets in Hand* (Puffin, 1985), reprinted by permission of the poet's executor, Patrick Walsh. Colin West, 'The Father Christmas on the Cake' from *The Big Book of Nonsense* (Hutchinson, 2001), copyright © the author, reprinted with his permission. Kit Wright, 'The Wicked Singers' from *Rabbiting One* (Collins, 1978), copyright © Kit Wright and reprinted with the author's permission. Samaritan's Purse International Ltd, stories and information from *Operation Christmas Child*. Extracts from *The Friday Miracle* (Puffin Books 1969), with permission from the Save the Children's Fund. Extracts from *Christmas Rhymes & Woodcuts for Children*, by J. Stewart Caulton, by permission of the Church Literature Association. 1930s Robertson's Golden Shred Mincemeat advertisement, by permission of Centura Foods. The letters and photographs of the Longfellow family are included by courtesy of the National Park Service, Longfellow National Historic Site in Cambridge, Massachusetts, USA.

Picture Credits

Quentin Blake, pp. 2, and 12, *Hogmanay and Tiffany* (Geoffrey Bles, 1970), copyright © Quentin Blake. Eve Garnett, p. 22, illustration originally published in *Is it well with the child?*